THE RISE AND FALL OF ENGLISH

The Rise and Fall of English
Reconstructing English as a Discipline

ROBERT SCHOLES

Yale University Press   New Haven and London

Published with assistance from the Louis Stern
Memorial Fund.

Designed by Sonia L. Scanlon.
Set in Adobe Garamond type by Tseng Information
Systems, Inc., Durham, North Carolina.
Printed in the United States of America by
Vail-Ballou Press, Binghamton, New York.

Library of Congress Cataloging-in-Publication Data
Scholes, Robert E.
The rise and fall of English : reconstructing .
English as a discipline / Robert Scholes.
p.   cm.
Includes bibliographical references and index.
ISBN 0-300-07151-5 (cloth : alk. paper)
ISBN 0-300-08084-0 (pbk. : alk. paper)
1. English philology—Study and teaching
(Higher)—United States.   2. English
philology—Study and teaching (Secondary)—
United States.   3. English philology—Study
and teaching—Great Britain.   4. English
philology—Study and teaching—Theory, etc.
5. English teachers—United States—
Biography.   6. Scholes, Robert E.   I. Title.
PE68.U5S35   1998
420'.71'173—dc21   97-21686

A catalogue record for this book is available from the
British Library.

To the teachers with whom I shared the experiences of the English Coalition and Pacesetter English. You have changed my life, and I will always be grateful to you for that.

CONTENTS

PREFACE

Once upon a time there was a boy who loved language. He loved it all: nursery rhymes, stories, comic books, plays, movies, advertising, instructions on packages, even schoolbooks. What becomes of such a boy? If he is lazy—and lucky—he becomes an English teacher. I was such a boy, and that is what became of me. This book is my attempt to explain—to myself and others—just what has happened to my chosen profession. It is also an attempt to pay back, to a profession that has given me a rewarding life, something of what I have received. In these pages I have tried to explain, to myself and others, how English attained its present place in our educational system (especially college education), to diagnose the symptoms of an educational illness that I occasionally call "hypocriticism," and to make recommendations, both general and specific, for a change of direction, a reconstruction of the field of English studies as a discipline.

Such an undertaking risks giving offense to many people who are concerned about the field in question. Even more, it risks boring those who want dramatic indictments and sweeping condemnations of conspiracies to betray Western Civilization as we have known it. The reality of the situation, however, does not lend itself to such dramatic representation. It is not a neat conspiracy but a muddle—and it takes patience and perseverance to sort out a muddle—even a muddle in a teapot, as any reader of tea leaves could tell us. Am I reading tea leaves? We shall see. In any case, I always try to read my texts as well as I can. In this particular case, though, I risk annoying both traditionalists and avant-gardists by adopting a militant middle position on many of the questions that currently vex English studies.

Nevertheless, I would accept the designation *radical* for this enterprise because I am truly interested in returning to the roots of English studies—and because I shall be advocating a massive change of direction for those studies. Radical in one sense, many readers of these pages may find me conservative in another, because I am critical of much that has been going on recently in the name of "theory," and because I believe that concepts like *truth* and *reality* are necessary for the health of a discipline called English. Others, I am sure, will see me as part of the great conspiracy to betray our way of life. But such political labels do not really matter, except to the extent that they may confuse things. What matters is the spirit in which the enterprise has been conducted. In this case, I believe, what matters is that the boy who loved language is still alive and well in the old man who has made his living by professing English and is now turning a well-disposed but critical eye on his profession. The old man still loves all the lively forms of expression and representation, verbal and visual, from epics and landscapes to cartoons and bumper stickers. What he has never learned, some would say, is "good taste." If this be true (and you will notice that he can use the subjunctive on serious occasions), then his experience must constitute the strongest evidence that an English education often fails to inculcate good taste, for some of the finest English teachers in the world have given him their best shot. (He is me, of course—or I, I suppose. O grammar! *O tempora, O mores!* as my friend Tully once remarked.)

The following five chapters are independent but interrelated essays. I begin with a historical discussion of the rise of English in two early American colleges, then examine aspects of what I describe as a fall or process of falling, and conclude with recommendations for changes aimed at making the fall a fortunate one. In between the chapters are "assignments," which were my responses to particular tasks that I agreed to undertake within the field of English during the time when I was considering the larger issues discussed in this book. It is my hope that these particular assignments will lend specificity to some of the more general concerns of the chapters. In some of them, and in other places in this book, I have not hesitated to bring my own experiences as a student and teacher of English into the picture.

Whether these experiences serve to enhance my credibility or diminish it, I must leave to my readers. In any case, it seemed necessary on some occasions to bear witness, or own up, to my personal stake in the matters under discussion. Everything in this book, I want to say unequivocally, is motivated by my love of the English language and my concern for the students who must learn to use it as well as they can. May they learn to love it as I have loved it, and may it serve them as well as it has me!

ACKNOWLEDGMENTS

As I have worked on this book over the past several years—and in particular, as I have tried to rethink, revise, and conclude it in the past few months—helpful books have often come to hand serendipitously. Some years ago the late Elmer Blistein gave me a copy of Walter Bronson's history of Brown University, which started me down the historical path I follow in Chapter 1. More recently, while escorting Marcus and Sarah Smith through the wonders of Warren, Rhode Island, where Brown began, the *Autobiography* of Billy Phelps literally fell into my hands from the shelves of an antique mall. Then, on a visit to Iowa City, I received much useful feedback from members of both the English and Education departments—and from John Gerber, the best department head I have ever seen, a copy of his history of the Iowa English Department. Even more recently my colleague Leonard Tennenhouse loaned me his copy of Franklin Court's book about the rise of English studies in British universities. To the authors of these books, as well as to the people who led me to them, I am grateful indeed—but there is no end to thanking the authors of books, so I will confine myself to mentioning those who have helped in other ways. For many conversations about these matters over the years, I must thank my frequent collaborator Nancy R. Comley. And for reading an earlier version of this book and making suggestions that were both drastic and acute, I am immensely grateful to my first friend in this profession, Carl H. Klaus, gardener extraordinaire and author of *My Vegetable Love.* Imperfect as my text may still be, it is better in many ways because of the guidance I received from this master of elegant prose and dedicated teacher of rhetoric and writing. Finally, I want to express my gratitude to Dan Heaton for a superb job of editing that went well beyond the call of duty.

As this book developed, many of these ideas were tested in print.

Though there is scarcely anything here that has not been rethought, rewritten, and rearranged, I am grateful to the editors of the following journals and volumes, who gave permission to recycle some of the material that appeared in their pages: *English Education; The South Central Review;* Bruce Henricksen and Thais E. Morgan, eds., *Reorientations: Critical Theories & Pedagogies* (Urbana: University of Illinois Press, 1990); Joseph Gibaldi, ed., *Introduction to Scholarship in Modern Languages and Literatures* (New York: Modern Language Association of America, 1992); John Clifford and John Schilb, eds., *Writing Theory and Critical Theory* (New York: Modern Language Association of America, 1994); Patricia A. Sullivan and Donna J. Qualley, eds., *Pedagogy in the Age of Politics: Reading and Writing (in) the Academy* (Urbana: National Council of Teachers of English, 1994); James F. Slevin and Art Young, eds., *Critical Theory and the Teaching of Literature: Politics, Curriculum, Pedagogy* (Urbana: National Council of Teachers of English, 1996); W. V. Harris, ed., *Beyond Poststructuralism* (State College: Pennsylvania State University Press, 1996).

THE RISE AND FALL OF ENGLISH

PAPAGENO: Mein Kind, was wurden wir nun sprechen?
PAMINA: Die Wahrheit!
            Die Wahrheit, sei sie auch Verbrechen!
                          Mozart/Schikaneder, *Die Zauberflöte*

PAPAGENO: My child, what shall we say this time?
PAMINA: The truth!
            The truth! Even if it were a crime!
                                        The Magic Flute

The Rise of English in Two American Colleges

About the past we can tell stories and write histories. Our own time, however, is a foreign country, whose customs are never clear to us. This is what Hegel had in mind when he observed that the owl of Minerva waits until twilight to take flight. In the present case, I will begin my historical narrative with some sense that many others would assent to the main features of my tale. Later, I shall be winging it into the confusing glare of contemporary debates, trying very hard to lose neither myself nor my readers as I go. In this chapter, however, I have a fairly simple story to tell, though it gets more complicated toward the end.

As my title suggests, it is a story about the rise of English as a field of study in two American colleges that I happen to know well. I believe, in fact, that what happened in these schools, though they were among the first American colleges, also happened at other schools, both private and public, that were established after them. John Gerber, in his recent book *The Teaching of English at the University of Iowa: The First Hundred Years, 1861–1961*, offers a similar pattern for the history of English studies at that school, for example. The pattern that I am about to describe, as the title of this book indicates, is a rise that contains within it the seeds and signs of a fall—a fall now discernible in college and university English departments across the country, and in the field of study as a whole. Whether or not this will be a fortunate fall remains to be determined. This book, especially Chapter 5, is an attempt to grasp fortune's forelock and write a happy ending beyond the ending for my story. Academic fields are not permanent. Other modes of study have risen and fallen over the years. The rise of English itself, in fact, is closely linked to the fall of

classical studies from a position of eminence and to the near oblit-
eration of rhetoric as a college subject.

Classical studies—Greek and Latin—were the backbone of the
humanistic curriculum in this country until about a century ago. In
their heyday it must have seemed as if they would go on forever. But
they fell, and when they did, the fall was astonishingly rapid. When
entrance requirements were relaxed at Yale, for instance, in just eight
years—from 1907 to 1914—the number of students entering the college with prior knowledge of Greek went from 98 percent to less
than 50 percent. In the same period the number of students elect-
ing to study Greek in their first year dropped from 60 percent to 29
percent, and in seven more years the number fell to a mere 8 percent (Pierson, 1952, 714–15). Many people thought that with such
changes the heavens, too, would fall. If they fell, it was not noticed.

In the story I shall tell, English rose rapidly at the end of the
nineteenth century and in the first decades of the twentieth. Its decline began after midcentury and now threatens to accelerate. How
far it may fall is still in doubt. English is not Greek, of course, and it
is bound to be a subject of interest as long as it is the dominant language of our country and a world language of major importance, but
it has not always been taught and studied in the forms we are accustomed to and sometimes believe to be eternal. In particular, English
literature (which is what most college and university professors of
English think of as "English") was scarcely visible in college curricula
before the middle of the nineteenth century. It assumed its central
place in the humanities curriculum for good historical reasons. If it
must now yield that place, it will be another case in which, as the
English tourist Haines says to Stephen Dedalus in *Ulysses,* it seems
that "history is to blame" (Joyce, 1961, 20).

The rise of English in American colleges is now a familiar part of
the story, thanks especially to such books as Richard Ohmann's *English in America* and Gerald Graff's *Professing Literature.* My version
of this story will be similar to theirs, but with some different em-

phases that enable me to propose another ending for this tale that is still in progress. To begin with, I see a slightly different version of the historical interactions between the studies we now call *literature* and *composition* and their predecessors: *rhetoric* or *oratory* and *belles lettres*. But let us begin at the beginning.

In the beginning there were no English professors. In 1701, when the Collegiate School was established in Saybrook, Connecticut, the entire staff consisted of the rector, who gave lectures, and a tutor, who supervised the students and their exercises. The tutor, with no more preparation than an undergraduate degree from Harvard—where else would you get one in 1701?—did the dirty work, while the rector pontificated. This division of labor, as may have occurred to you, is still with us: pontification at the top and overworked, under-prepared instruction at the bottom. There was a rapid turnover among the tutors, then as now. They also multiplied in number, then as now. In its first two decades of existence the Collegiate School moved to New Haven, acquired some books, money, and a family name from a rich nabob named Elihu Yale; fifty years later it had an enrollment of seventy or so students and a teaching faculty that consisted of the rector and three tutors. In 1767, English grammar, language, and composition were introduced by the tutors, who taught these subjects. In 1768 a literary and debating society was established by the students. In 1776 instruction in belles lettres was offered to the seniors, along with history—by a tutor. In 1817 a Professorship of Rhetoric and Oratory was established. By then there had already been established Professorships of Divinity (1754), Mathematics and Natural Philosophy (1770), Ecclesiastical History (1777), Law (1801), Chemistry and Natural History (1802), and Hebrew, Greek, and Latin (1805).

The Professorship of Rhetoric and Oratory, as we have seen, was instituted at Yale in 1817. In the evolution of this chair can be read the fortunes of English as a field of study. In 1839 its title was changed to Rhetoric and the English Language, and in 1863 to Rhetoric and English Literature. Thus, only a little more than a century ago did literature achieve equal status with rhetoric on the faculty of Yale College, and what happened at Yale was happening in other colleges as well. (For the Yale curriculum in 1822–23, see Appendix A.) We can, for instance, compare Rhode Island College, which was founded in 1764, more than a half-century after Yale, but developed along similar lines. In 1803 the corporation of this school voted "that the donation of $5000 Dollars, if made to this College within one Year from the late Commencement, shall entitle the donor to name the College" (Bronson, 155). In 1804 a graduate of Rhode Island College named Nicholas Brown offered the required sum. He made the offer in these terms: "I hereby make a Donation of Five Thousand Dollars to Rhode Island College to remain to perpetuity as a fund for the establishment of a Professorship of *Oratory & Belles Letters*" (*sic,* Bronson, 156). In changing its name, the college also changed its designation, becoming not Brown College but Brown University. The new university, after the donation had gathered interest for a few years, established a chair that included belles lettres before its rivals in Massachusetts and Connecticut did, for the Boylston Professorship at Harvard (1803) was in Rhetoric and Oratory, as was the chair established at Yale in 1817.

But what did Oratory and Belles Letters actually mean? This combination of topics dates from the lectures on them by Adam Smith and Hugh Blair in the Scottish universities during the eighteenth century (Court, chapter 1). It meant something different to Smith than it did to Blair, as Franklin E. Court has persuasively demonstrated, but in both of their courses it involved the use of English literature not as an end in itself but in the service of verbal decorum, morality, or taste. At Brown as at Yale, such literature as was studied got treated in a similar way. The grammar of the language received some attention, and the rhetoric of public address was covered extensively, both in its classical forms (Cicero's orations and *De Oratore* and Longinus's *On the Sublime*) and in such eighteenth-century texts as Ward's *System of Oratory* and Sheridan's *Lectures on Elocu-*

tion. Formal logic also contributed to what was clearly a curriculum designed to prepare graduates for careers in the church or for participation in civil government, both of which depended heavily upon oratory.

Though all the students were required to write, their compositions were designed as orations, some of which they were expected to memorize and deliver before an audience (Bronson, 104–5). In fact, the orientation of this teaching was so resolutely oral that little attention was paid to such niceties as spelling, a matter that shocked Walter Bronson when (in 1914) he looked into the written texts of the early graduates of what was then Rhode Island College: "When we examine their spelling, grammar, and other beggarly elements, it is something of a shock to find that these students, of native American stock and of classical nurture, are far from impeccable" (122). We might dilate on Bronson's use of the word *beggarly.* In his context it refers to what we would call accidentals—the parts of a written text that are not substantive—but the word also catches his desire to trivialize the issue and his disgust that it is an issue at all. He clearly wishes that student writing were "impeccable," but just as clearly he resents being responsible for the achievement of such necessary but trivial impeccability. He returns to this theme when quoting from the valedictory address given at the college's first commencement, the written text of which exhibits a series of wildly original spellings that left Bronson, who was still teaching English at Brown himself in 1914, shaking his head: "Modern teachers of English," he observed, "when weary with cropping the hydra heads of bad spelling and bad grammar, may at least comfort themselves with the thought that their dragon foe is of ancient lineage" (124). As the "laws" of 1783 themselves suggest (see Appendix B), no one at that time paid much attention to spelling. The laws themselves offer nonstandard spellings of several of the prescribed authors' names.

These, let us remember, were the good old days, and what we learn from them is that from 1770 to 1914 and right on to the present moment, English teachers have not found any method to ensure that graduates of their courses would use what were considered to be correct grammar and spelling. A number of conclusions can be drawn from this situation. One is that the good old days when students wrote "correctly" never existed. A second conclusion might well be that two hundred years of failure are sufficient to demonstrate that what Bronson called beggarly matters are both impossible to teach and not really necessary for success in life. We may well be contemplating two hundred years of wasted effort—except that there is no evidence that the teachers of two centuries ago really cared much about how writing looked. They were oriented to the oral performance itself and regarded the written texts primarily as rough drafts of the real thing: the oration.

Here, for instance, is a picture of the essential part of education in the later eighteenth century. A successful graduate of Rhode Island College is discussing his training under Presidents Manning and Maxcy:

> It was not the Philosophy of Rhetoric, (falsely so called,) which in their time, gave lustre to instructions; it was Rhetoric itself; the divine art of persuasion, which, on their tongues, inspired their disciples with the desire to imitate, and the hope to resemble them. . . . You all remember the elevated advanced stage where the speaker took his stand, when, under supervision of the whole authority, surrounded by the entire collegiate assembly, awed by the continued and pervading spirit of the hour and the occasion, he gave voice to his own, as soon as the last echo of the voice of devotion had ceased to whisper in the ear of the listening audience. It was not to the assembled Greeks, it was not at the Olympic Games that he spoke; but the pupil, who passed through this ordeal, under the

> eye of Manning or Maxcy, has never since that time,
> with more anxiety prepared himself for any other; or
> gone through it with more fear and trembling. . . .
> In belles lettres and eloquence, where was the insti-
> tution in our country, the character of which stood
> more permanently distinguished. (Bronson, 137)

It is plain from these words of Tristram Burges, who represented
Rhode Island in Congress and later taught at Brown himself, that the
climax of education in the college curriculum of his time was the moment when each student took the podium to deliver an oration under
the watchful eyes of men who were themselves admired for the eloquence of their own oratory. Burges calls these performances "belles
lettres and eloquence," and the linking of the two terms to describe
an oratorical performance is itself significant. In these orations the
rhetorical power of persuasion and the aesthetic power of literature
are conceived as one thing, not differentiated as we regularly differen-
tiate them but seen as a unified power to move and stir an audience
with language. Listen, for a moment, to the youthful Burges himself,
in his commencement oration of 1796, speaking of the imagination
whose verbal form he called eloquence and belles lettres:

> By imagination, man seems to verge towards creative
> power. Aided by this, he can perform all the won-
> ders of sculpture and painting. He can almost make
> the marble speak. He can almost make the brook
> murmur down the painted landscape. Often on the
> pinions of imagination, he soars aloft where the eye
> has never traveled; where other stars glitter on the
> mantle of night, and a more effulgent sun lights up
> the blushes of morning. Flying from world to world,
> he gazes on all the glories of creation: or, lighting
> on the distant margin of the universe, darts the eye
> of fancy over the mighty void, where power creative

> never yet has energized, where existence still sleeps in
> the wide of abyss of possibility. (Bronson, 139)

This rhetoric, which may quite technically be called sublime, dates from 1796, let us remember. Here we can see what later came to be called Romanticism evolving out of a curriculum that gave serious attention to Longinus on the sublime. Burges is also abundantly aware of the chapters on "Grandeur and Sublimity" and "Beauty of Language" in Lord Kames's *Elements of Criticism,* which was a part of the college curriculum. In this connection it is worth noting that what Kames meant by criticism is not what we mean by it today. His vastly influential book was a treatise on aesthetics and a rhetoric all in one. What he meant by criticism was the rational study or science of the fine arts and the emotions associated with them, a topic that would later be taken up by Kant in the *Critique of Judgment* and by Schelling and Hegel in their lectures on the fine arts. For our purposes, however, the important thing to note is that for students who studied Kames, and especially for those at Rhode Island College who studied him along with Longinus, oratory and belles lettres were one indivisible thing. An oration, under this regime, was meant to be both moving and a beautiful object in its own right. This, obviously, is the ideal animating the valedictorian of 1796. He meant to be eloquent in a culture that valued oral rhetoric above all other modes of language.

It is hard for us to conceive of this older attitude toward rhetoric, but we may get some idea of it by reading a letter written to the editor of the Charleston (South Carolina) *City Gazette* in July 1819, by someone who had heard Jonathan Maxcy give a Fourth of July oration a few days before. (Maxcy had left Rhode Island and become the first president of South Carolina College in 1802.)

> Last Sunday we went to hear Dr. Maxcy. It being
> the 4th of July, it was a discourse appropriate to that
> eventful period. I had always been led to believe the

Doctor an eloquent and impressive preacher; but had no idea, till now, that he possessed such transcendent powers. I never heard such a stream of eloquence— It flowed from his lips, even like the oil from Aaron's beard. Every ear was delighted, every heart elated, every bosom throbbed with gratitude. . . . I was sometimes in pain, lest this good man should outdo himself and become exhausted; but as he advanced in his discourse, he rose in animation, till at length he reached flights the most sublime, and again descended with the same facility with which he soared. . . . In short, I never heard anything to compare to Dr. Maxcy's sermon in the course of all my life; and old as I am, I would now walk even twenty miles through the hottest sands to listen to such another discourse. I am persuaded I shall never hear such another in my life. (Bronson, 133)

In the good old days, before there were professors of English, there were teachers of oratory and belles lettres who themselves practiced belletristic oratory. They did what they taught and they taught what they did. No wonder they were respected by those who came to learn from them. History, with its notorious dialectical cunning, undid all this. (For a chronicle of the demise of rhetoric at Brown, see Appendix C.) At first the changes came slowly and hesitantly. There were no drastic alterations in the curricula of American colleges until the closing decades of the nineteenth century. Then they were precipitated by the success of Charles W. Eliot in opening the Harvard curriculum. Coming to Harvard from MIT in 1870, Eliot began at once a struggle to allow Harvard students a greater choice of courses. Resistance was fierce and prolonged, but by 1884 he had won his battle. His new "elective system" set Harvard on the road to being a truly great university. What Eliot did was to change study at Harvard

College from a rigidly prescribed set of courses, with a few choices built in during the last year or so, to a virtually total freedom of choice among the existing possibilities. This enabled the needs and desires of students to have a real effect on the curriculum, which began to change drastically from that moment. The changes that Eliot instituted were imitated widely, partly because Harvard was admired but even more because these were the changes that a changing world required. They were also the changes that allowed English as we know it to establish itself in the curriculum of college after college.

Meanwhile, at other schools, the development of "English" took other, but parallel, forms. At Yale a course called English Literature and Disputation joined the required freshman courses in Greek, Latin, and mathematics in 1876. At that time, these two terms of English and Disputation were all the English offered in the Yale curriculum, as opposed to sixteen term hours in Greek and sixteen in Latin. When Yale went to a modified elective system in 1883, twelve term courses in English were available. By 1889, Yale offered more courses in English than in Latin and twice as many as in Greek. A revolution had taken place.

At Brown things went a bit more slowly, but the story is a similar one. It is the story of how oratory (with its belletristic flourishes) dwindled into rhetoric, and rhetoric gradually lost its oral emphasis, finally giving way to the exclusively written focus of English composition. The proud tradition of oratory as a fine art was dead at Brown, and by the turn of the century the old rhetoric department had been swallowed up by the English department. In 1905, what had been courses in the composition of speeches became just plain composition. But without oratory as their subject matter, the new courses in composition began to flounder. Many of them turned to literature for their subject matter. This meant that the written texts produced by students were of a vastly different kind from the imaginative texts studied in class. Instead of reading orations and producing oratory, students began to read literature and produce criticism—and the stage was set for the twentieth-century developments in the field of English. This same process, of course, had transformed the students from producers of work comparable to what they studied into passive consumers of texts they could never hope to emulate—changing the teacher into a middleman, huckster, or priestly exegete.

The English department as we know it was in place in the first decade of this century at Brown, Yale, and many other schools across the country. All that happened in the ensuing decades was growth, as former Greek and Latin students joined the former rhetoric students in English courses. Along with growth came increasing specialization and professionalization, as the doctorate and Germanic methods began to dominate instruction. Professionalization took curricular form first as philology, then as New Criticism, and later as "theory." The development of philology was driven by two different but related motives. One, under the influence of German linguistic scholarship, was the attempt to be more "scientific" and "Germanic"—and this was not without a whiff of Aryan racism. The other was the need to compete with classical studies and the sciences in terms of the mental rigor that such study was supposed to produce in its students. Both of these motives served to add intellectual stiffening to a curriculum that was really based on what we might call the Story of English Literature, a simple chronological tale, broken down into periods. The New Criticism, on the other hand, was an attempt to generate a rigor that was not scientific but distinctly humanistic. Later developments show the pendulum swinging back and forth, as structuralism veered toward science and poststructuralist theory back toward an antiscientific point of view.

Meanwhile, the story kept getting longer, of course, since literature kept getting written, but it also got simpler, becoming a tale of lofty imaginative achievements. We will do well to pause here, for a moment, and consider the fortunes of the word *literature* itself in the history of English. When Juan Luis Vives, the sixteenth-century humanist, proposed the study of vernacular literatures in 1531, he included in that category "books in law, geography, and history" (Court, 10). And in the early curricula of American colleges, writers like Bacon and Locke loomed large, though they soon dropped out of sight. The concept of belles lettres, as developed in the eighteenth century, served as a transition, then, from an older view of literature as including all kinds of written works worthy of study, to a different view that led to a curriculum dominated by Romantic notions of genius and imagination, along with their Arnoldian development as "high seriousness." This historical shift in emphasis, from literature as simply good books, to belles lettres as eloquent prose, to literature as imaginative high seriousness, is clearly reflected in the changing curricula of American colleges during the past two centuries.

The curricular transition from oratory to the study of imaginative literature was negotiated more successfully by some English professors than others. Those who were most successful as teachers were the ones who managed to put their oratorical fervor at the service of literary texts. One of those who best exemplifies this successful transition, and the resistance it encountered, is William Lyon Phelps. From the career of Phelps we can learn much about what the study of English was like at its peak of influence and prestige—and also much about why this could not be sustained. Phelps attended Yale as an undergraduate from 1883 to 1887 and taught English there from 1892 to 1933. Here is a significant passage from his *Autobiography with Letters* (1939): "I shall never forget the afternoon in my father's house when I read *Maud* for the first time. I entered the room one kind of man and left it another kind of man. . . . I shall always be grateful to this poem, for it was the means of my conversion; I escaped from the gall of bitterness and the bond of Philistine iniquity, into the kingdom of light. And after all, it is a great poem" (Phelps, 145).

Billy Phelps (as he was affectionately called—and liked to be called—by his students) can mark for us the apogee of English as an academic field. He had retired by the time I got to Yale as a freshman in 1946, but his influence was still felt, even as the rising tide of the New Criticism was beginning to displace his brand of ethical enthusiasm with a more technical (or professional) way of reading. That New Critical tide, however, barely lapped at the edges of the courses I took, which were mostly taught by men whose careers had begun while Billy was still teaching. When my professor of Romanticism told us how Wordsworth's poetry had comforted him in the trenches during the Great War, he was speaking, as he knew, to many of my classmates who had just come back from a greater one, but he spoke in the tradition of Billy Phelps, and his students still responded to that way of teaching. Nor am I about to claim exemption for myself from such sentiments, for I can remember only too clearly what it was like to sit in a convertible under a tree, mourning a lost love, and taking comfort from the poems of, yes, Tennyson. Moreover, when I sailed off to defend "democracy" in Korea, I took a short anthology of poetry with me on the trip. My conviction that things have changed, then, is accompanied by a definite sense of loss, but I do not think nostalgia is a useful guide for action. My point is that what I am calling the fall of English has gone on mainly during my watch. I am implicated. This book is part of a long effort of extrication.

The heights from which English has been falling were first climbed by Billy Phelps and others like him at various schools in this country around the turn of the nineteenth century. The fall itself has been the product of changes in the modern world and of changes in the field itself. Within the field of study certain crucial changes may well be the result of mirroring too closely that larger world rather than devising a thoughtful response to those external changes. Whatever the exact mix may have been, it is this combination of external and internal developments that has led to our present situation, which is so different from that of our illustrious predecessor, Billy Phelps. In the history of English as a field of study, Phelps represents a moment between philology and New Criticism, a moment when it was indeed possible to profess literature with evangelical fervor. But that moment has passed. It cannot be recuperated now. We may be able to understand our situation more fully, however, by considering Phelps's view of his own professional career.

The epiphany represented by Billy's first encounter with Tennyson's *Maud* may well be a fictionalized compression of a more gradual process, but it can also tell us something genuine about what literature—poetry in particular—represented for him. We need to ask, however, what he meant by entering the "kingdom of light"? Actually, he was reading the poem because it was one of twelve possible topics for an essay that the entire sophomore class was required to write. His contribution got him one of the four first prizes, which led to an invitation to write for the *Yale Literary Magazine*—and so to his entire career. But he presents this experience to us (without concealing in any way the other aspects of it) as a "conversion." A conversion, we must ask, to what? The answer he supplies is that he came to realize "in that moment the significance of poetry; that the poet is the interpreter for us of the beauty of nature and the passions of man" (Phelps, 145). This revelation is less than startling. It had been a commonplace for a century or so when Billy uttered it. For this reason it seems inadequate to explain the fervor induced by the experience, and this inadequacy leads us to look for an interpretation beyond the one that Phelps provides us. The key, I believe, lies in another quotation from his autobiography: "In the Baptist denomination one could receive a preaching license from one's church; so a few months after graduation, I went to Hartford, preached a trial sermon in the Asylum Avenue Baptist Church, and was given a license to preach" (Phelps, 199).

The experience recorded here—of how he became a Baptist preacher—should confirm for us the connection between Billy's experience of poetry and his second vocation: a Christian ministry. The language he uses to describe his experience while reading Tennyson is saturated with religion. In it he recounts the story of a conversion leading from Philistine darkness to the kingdom of light. But the experience of becoming a preacher is couched in the language of business—obtaining a license to preach. This is the era of Bruce Barton, in which Christ was often thought of as a sort of Rotarian (as in James Joyce's story "Grace"), but, once again, I do not think mockery of Phelps is going to be helpful. What is important here is that, for this representative figure of the professional high-water mark of English as a field of study, there is absolutely no tension between teaching and preaching. They are aspects of the same calling. And this, I believe, is the reason for the joy that animates Billy's new experience of poetry. He did not have to choose between vocations, because by choosing poetry and literature in general, he could, in effect, choose preaching as well. He was, of course a white, Anglo-Saxon, Protestant male teaching/preaching to a student body that had been constructed in his own image—or he in its. I am not joking. When I entered Yale in 1946, I learned, from a sociology professor, that, by some strange coincidence, Yale's entering classes consisted regularly of 10 percent Jews, 10 percent Roman Catholics like myself, and 80 percent Protestants. In Phelps's day the ratio of Protestants to others must have been even higher.

For my present purposes, however, this is less important than the close relationship between Christianity and literature: the conviction, so obviously held by Phelps, that literature offered quasi-sacred texts that could be expounded by a licensed teacher/preacher to reveal the entrance to the kingdom of light. The first professor of English language and literature in England, it should be noted—Thomas Dale, appointed at University College, London, in 1828—was a practicing minister who saw his role as using literary texts to inculcate Christian virtues. It is worth noticing, perhaps, that he was quickly fired and the position soon shifted to the new philology, partly because entrenched classicists saw his courses in English literature as a threat to their own hegemony (Court, 59–67). How right they were! In 1892 at Yale, however, the power of philology was waning and with it the power of classics. But Billy's way at Yale was not smooth, mainly because he was not simply a gifted orator/preacher among the philologists; he was also a curricular innovator, who met with considerable resistance from the senior faculty:

> I began work as a full-time Instructor in English at Yale in the Autumn of 1892. The College was nearly two hundred years old, but this was the first time that English literature had ever been taught to Freshmen. . . .
>
> One day in the Spring of 1895 I called on Professor Beers and told him that I should like to give a course on Modern Novels, confining the subject-matter entirely to contemporary works. . . . Thus was inaugurated what I believe was the first course in any university in the world confined wholly to contemporary fiction. I called the course *Modern Novels*. It was open to Seniors and Juniors, and was elected by two hundred and fifty men. . . . Although the undergraduates apparently enjoyed both the course and the writing of a weekly critical theme, which I made obligatory, and although the newspaper comment was on the whole highly favorable, the majority of the older professors gave me to understand that unless I dropped the course at the end of its first year, I should myself be dropped from the faculty. . . . Then the Dean of the college, Henry P. Wright, sent for me and made the following remark: "If your course had been a failure there would have been no objection to its continuance." (Phelps, 279, 297–98, 301)

Two hundred and fifty students represented a sizable chunk of the total undergraduate population of Yale College in 1895. Clearly, there was a hunger among the students for the kind of course Billy wanted to teach, and, just as clearly, they liked the way he taught. It should be added that no one has given us a more damning picture of the opposition between scholarship and teaching at an institution like Yale than Billy Phelps: "There was a blight, a curse on the teaching, unfortunate both for teachers and pupils. Instructors who were thirty years old had the classroom manner of old men. . . . These men certainly gave no indication of enjoying teaching; and of course the students found no joy in the learning" (Phelps, 282). Phelps, and others like him, enabled English departments in this country to take advantage of the opportunity offered by the decline of classics. And many English departments took advantage of this opportunity for a while, by putting teaching first, ahead of scholarship. Billy published a good deal himself, but later he acknowledged that he had wasted his time doing respectable scholarly editions and frankly admitted that much of his published work belonged to what he regarded as his third calling, after teaching and preaching: journalism. Even in his writing, he saw himself as a popularizer, a teacher, and, of course, a preacher.

Billy Phelps loved teaching, made friends of his students, and fired them with his own enthusiasm for literature. At the same time he was convinced that the study of literature prepared them well for success in business and the other professions open to them when they graduated. He believed that the study of literature would help his students to become better fathers, husbands, sons, brothers, and friends (he taught only men at Yale in those days, of course), but he also thought that literary studies would give them a knowledge of human nature, a "sympathy, tolerance, and understanding"—which he saw as assets "for success in any calling where one comes into contact with people" (Phelps, 309). One would not like to argue that he was wrong about this. All the same, the comfortable assurance that a richer, fuller humanity would be an asset in business, law, or politics is not so easy to retain in our present world, even if one were certain that the study of literature, as it is presently conducted, would indeed lead to such an enhanced humane culture.

I am suggesting that the qualities now required for success in business and professional life have become further removed from those that Phelps believed literary study might develop. I had a *Maud* experience in my own undergraduate life which may throw some light on what has happened. My *Maud* was not the poetry of Tennyson that I wallowed in lugubriously among the pangs of erotic rejection—it was Arthur Miller's *Death of a Salesman* on Broadway, whither I had been dispatched from New Haven to see whether this new work could indeed meet the exacting academic standard for "true tragedy." I cannot remember the verdict on that count, but the play shook me down to my shoes, because it represented a business and family life so close to my own experience that it drove me to face, however briefly, the actual conditions and possibilities of my own existence. More than any other single experience, it changed my life and started me on the path I have since followed. A conversion experience, indeed—an experience, though, that revealed not a convergence between my literary training and the business world but a terrifying divergence of values. This gap, between the values of the humanities and those of the powerful worlds of business and public life, has only increased in the decades since *Death of a Salesman* appeared. And our inability to deal with it has been a contributing cause to our present state of confusion.

What I am trying to do in this book is work through the very complex situation of a field of study that seems to me hollow, falling, though perhaps not yet visibly fallen. I shall also try to offer solutions, at various levels, to the problems I discern. But this fall is a very complicated matter, which will occupy us for several chapters. As I understand it, the fall of English is partly the result of cultural shifts that are beyond the power of English departments to change—though not beyond their power of creative response. The fall is also a result of changes within the field of English itself, and these lie even more securely within our powers of response—if we can admit that we need to change our ways. At this point I shall just touch briefly on what I take to be the major external or social changes that have affected the field of English, for it would take an entire and quite different book to treat them fully, before returning to the changes within the field, which are themselves far from simple.

The external changes that bear most directly on the function of English as a field of study have to do with the position of literature itself in American culture. To put it simply, that quasi-religious status once accorded English literature by a class of individuals whose background was mainly privileged and Anglo-Germanic is hardly viable any longer. Two world wars and the Holocaust have had something to do with that, demonstrating powerfully that high culture is not necessarily a guarantee of the "sympathy, tolerance, and understanding" that Phelps believed it to be. The rise of a popular culture distributed through the mass media has also modified the textual equation. And one could point to important changes in the publishing industry, especially in the marketing and distribution of printed books and other texts. Men and women of letters, whether in or outside of the academy, have a reduced stature today in comparison to major figures in the film and television world. Young people who once wanted to be Hemingway (and many did), now want to be Scorsese, Spike Lee, or Spielberg. Moreover, a knowledge of English literary history is simply not the password to managerial and professional positions that it may once have been. Which is another way of saying that what happened to Greek and Latin is now happening to English. What this society *wants* of those who graduate from its schools and colleges with degrees in the humanities—as opposed to what many of those who claim to speak for it *say* it wants—are, at worst, docility and grammatical competence, at best, reliability and a high level of textual skills. What this society does *not* want from our educational institutions is a group of people imbued with critical skills and values that are frankly antagonistic to those that prevail in our marketplaces, courts, and legislative bodies.

This is, obviously, a problem of great weight and complexity. If the culture itself is sick, how should we prepare students to live in it and maintain a state of ethical health? How, that is, can English studies help students become fit for life in a world like ours? These questions will be addressed more fully in Chapters 4 and 5 and Assignment 4. For the moment, I wish only to point out that there is a serious gap between literary and artistic values, on the one hand, and the commercial and competitive values that are active in our society, on the other. From the viewpoint of the field of English this conflict can be seen in terms of the long struggle between literature and rhetoric for cultural dominance. Now, and the signs of it are everywhere, the pendulum is swinging back to rhetoric. Not only is our world dominated by political and advertising rhetoric, but literary texts themselves now appear to us more and more as instances of interested rather than disinterested language. The distance between Shakespeare's *Richard III* and Oliver Stone's *Nixon* turns out to be less great than one might have expected. And *Death of a Salesman,* too, was and is rhetoric: a tendentious, interested, persuasive, and beautiful text. This external change requires that we rethink the very concepts of rhetoric and literature in order to reinvent ourselves and our discipline. By "reinvent" I do not mean capitulation to a valueless regime of "spin" and "hype." I mean that we must rethink the relationship between textual representations of all kinds and the things that are represented in those texts. And that is part of what I shall be attempting in this book, too.

This vast and powerful cultural shift, which I have described with almost savage brevity here, has been driven by forces outside the academy. Other and related changes, however, have occurred within the walls. In schools, colleges, and elite universities, student bodies have changed from the relatively homogeneous group of Christian males encountered by Phelps to a much more heterogeneous gathering of races, religions, and genders. Faculties have changed in similar ways. Along with these changes in the academic population have come other changes, of which I shall enumerate just two that seem especially important:

(1) English is now a foreign literature in a (relatively) familiar language. In the United States, American literature is assuming the central place among several Anglophone literatures, displacing the literature of England itself. The literature of this foreign country, England, now requires formal preparation in the background of English history and culture, just as the study of French literature requires the study of France. To give a concrete instance, where the *Book of Common Prayer* could once be assumed as part of the intellectual equipment of most students, now it must be part of the English curriculum, if all the literary texts that borrow from it—even including such American works as Ernest Hemingway's *In Our Time* —are to be understood. We can no longer take it for granted that the literature of England (as opposed to literatures in English) should be the center of English studies. And if we choose to make it the center, we must recognize that such study needs more intellectual support than it used to require.

(2) Literature in general, which once seemed to be an end in itself because it led directly to transcendental virtues ("the kingdom of light"), is now seen, both positively and negatively, as politically interested. That is, literature, which once represented universal values, is now seen as representing values that are more local, historical, connected to particular times and places, to particular groups and their interests. Individuals—both faculty and students—who identify themselves as members of oppressed minori-

ties are drawn to texts that adequately represent them
and their struggles. And there are few in these times
who do not claim such status. Literature may still
lead to virtue, but because virtue itself is now seen in
social and political terms, different literary texts become means to different virtuous ends. This, which is
another aspect of the shift from literature to rhetoric,
is both a problem and an opportunity for English as
a field of study.

In later chapters I will suggest some appropriate responses to these
changed conditions of instruction. For the moment, however, I must
concentrate on trying to describe certain more technical shifts that
have occurred within the field itself during the past several decades.
These are aspects of a process of professionalization, which has had
both good and bad effects, but now stands in need of serious recon-
sideration.

When the twentieth century arrived, teachers like Billy Phelps
were drawing strength, either overtly or tacitly, from the powerful attempt of Matthew Arnold to replace dogma with literature. Billy's
mode of evangelical literary interpretation was not simply a personal
preference, though it was that, it was also a method underwritten by
the enormous authority of Arnold as an educator and cultural critic.
In our own time, however, another licensed preacher/professor has
made it impossible to continue accepting Arnold's values as transcendental in the way that teachers like Phelps understood them to be.
Northrop Frye, one of the finest teachers and literary theoreticians of
our own time, took a careful look at Arnold's famous "touchstones"
of literary value in his *Anatomy of Criticism* (1957), and found there
not transcendental or universal values but the values of a particular
social class in the service of an attempt to replace scripture with literature. Many have echoed Frye's discovery, but no one has said it
better. Let us attend to him:

When we examine the touchstone technique in Arnold, however, certain doubts arise about his motivation. The line from *The Tempest,* "In the dark backward and abysm of time," would do very well as a touchstone line. One feels that the line "Yet a tailor might scratch her where'er she did itch" somehow would not do, though it is equally Shakespearean and equally essential to the same play. (An extreme form of the same kind of criticism would, of course, deny this and insist that the line had been interpolated by a vulgar hack.) Some principle is clearly at work here which is much more highly selective than a purely critical experience of the play would be.

Here we should pause to notice that Frye's notion of a "purely critical experience" conserves much of the Arnoldian project—which remains at the center of our present critical debates. We shall return to this. But first, let us continue with Frye's next paragraph:

Arnold's "high seriousness" evidently is closely connected with the view that epic and tragedy, because they deal with ruling-class figures and require the high style of decorum, are the aristocrats of literary forms. All his Class One touchstones are from, or judged by the standards of, epic and tragedy. Hence his demotion of Chaucer and Burns to Class Two seems to be affected by a feeling that comedy and satire should be kept in their proper place, like the moral standards and the social classes which they symbolize. We begin to suspect that the literary judgments are projections of social ones. Why does Arnold *want* to rank poets? He says that we increase our admiration for those who manage to stay in Class One after we have made it very hard for them to do

so. This being clearly nonsense, we must look further.
When we read "in poetry the distinction between
excellent and inferior . . . is of paramount importance . . . because of the high destinies of poetry," we
begin to get a clue. We see that Arnold is trying to
create a new scriptural canon out of poetry to serve
as a guide for those social principles which he wants
culture to take over from religion. (Frye, 21–22)

Like so much in that extraordinary book of Frye's, these crucial paragraphs opened the way to all our subsequent discussions and disputes
about the literary canon and the field of English. In particular, Frye
made literary scholars and critics aware of two things that had been
overlooked or concealed during the academic hegemony of the New
Criticism. First, that "literary judgments are projections of social
ones" (though he tried to reserve for himself a field of "purely critical
experience"). And second, that the Arnoldian tradition in criticism
involved "trying to create a new scriptural canon out of poetry." The
way we now use the word *canon* in literary studies is very much the
way we learned to use it from Northrop Frye. And it was also Frye,
who—when very few students of literature thought of calling their
enterprise literary theory—told us that "the theory of literature is as
primary a humanistic and liberal pursuit as its practice" (20).

But we are getting ahead of ourselves, as can happen when one
tries to tell a complicated tale. Frye followed the New Criticism and
opened the way to structuralism, but a structuralism that maintained
its own sympathy with the Arnoldian project. What remains to be
shown is the relationship between the New Criticism and the evangelical Arnoldianism of Billy Phelps. Here, once again, Yale can serve
as the example of changes that took place across the whole spectrum
of higher education. I have been emphasizing Yale and Brown because these are places I know from the inside, but there are other
reasons for this emphasis. Yale, in particular, has been a leader in the

shifts of interest and method that have dominated the field in recent years. Both the New Criticism and deconstruction came to the rest of this country's English departments by way of Yale primarily—and Yale New Criticism and Yale deconstructionism both retained undercurrents of the Christian faith of Billy Phelps. This, which is by no means the received view of this bit of intellectual history, is a crucial point that will obviously take some explaining.

The first part of this explanation—that is, the nature of the link between New Criticism and Christianity—has already been argued persuasively by John Guillory in "The Ideology of Canon-Formation: T. S. Eliot and Cleanth Brooks," an essay that traces the path from Eliot's reconstruction of the canon of English literature in his early essays to the institutional underwriting of that very canon by the New Critics through such books as Brooks's *Modern Poetry and the Tradition* (1939) and *The Well-Wrought Urn* (1947). In this elegant essay Guillory shows how the New Criticism, rather than rejecting the Christian core of English as an evangelical enterprise, functioned as a subtle and more attractive alternative to Matthew Arnold's attempt to replace dogma with literature. He does this by reminding us that what Eliot's essays suggested and the New Critics instituted was the replacement of *doxa* with paradox. Under this regime, canonical texts were seen not as repositories of truth and beauty or touchstones of high seriousness but as embodiments of a discourse so ambiguous that it could not be debased and applied to any practical or dogmatic end. The study and teaching of the new canon of specifically noncognitive texts would of necessity fall to those trained not to extract truth from these texts but to show that they are canonical precisely because they resist any such reduction to *doxa* or dogma.

Those who understood this, either as teachers or students, became members of what Guillory calls a "marginal elite," an elite based upon a canon of texts that aspired neither to scientific nor didactic status but to a literary purity defined explicitly as the absence of such ambitions:

Nevertheless, literary culture has aspired to canonical consensus, an illusion reinforced by the cognitive
silence of the literary work, the silencing of difference. Very simply, canonical authors are made to *agree*
with one another; the ambiguity of literary language
means nothing less than the *univocity* of the canon.
I now want to examine this rule of canonical self-
identity as it governs the institutional dissemination
of literature. Eliot's fantasy of orthodoxy passes into
the university both as an ideology of the marginal
elite and as an instruction in the marginal relation of
the poem to truth. (Guillory, 350)

To document his case, Guillory looks at Cleanth Brooks's crucial
treatment of Donne's poem "The Canonization." He sees Brooks as
basing the poem's canonical status as poetry upon its ability to offer
and to inhabit a realm removed from and "above" the world of power
and cognitive assertion:

The ideological function of Brooks' reading concerns the demarcation of a spiritual realm between
the crudities of power and the crudities of fact. The
spiritual realm is *defined* by the audience the essay
addresses: the auditors are conceived at a moment
of apostolic succession, at just the moment of transition between Eliot and Brooks, as representative
figures of literary culture. The *incognito* clergy is re-
located within a *visible* social structure: the pedagogical institution. The idealized reading of the lovers'
withdrawal must be understood as symptomatic of
the professional commitment to the preservation of
value: just as the lovers institute love in their act of renunciation, so it is the marginality of value which is

both deplored and established by the idealization of literature. (356)

As he has observed earlier in the essay, "in teaching the canon, we are not only investing a set of texts with authority; we are equally instituting the authority of the teaching profession" (351). This is a terribly important point. Guillory is arguing—and I entirely agree with him about this—that the New Criticism functioned to construct for literature a safe place outside the pressures of the marketplace and the strict demands of scientific study (and above the realm of politics and social strife as well) in a lofty sphere of Arnoldian "disinterestedness." This realm was also, as he points out, a safe haven for professors, who had become a clergy without a dogma, teaching sacred texts without a God. This meant that, as universities became more and more driven by their professional schools and their links to a technological system of values and rewards, literature departments, and especially departments of English literature, represented the last, purest bastion of liberal education. Under this regime, the study of English was as "disinterested" as Matthew Arnold himself could have wished, but on firmer ground, the ground of literariness itself, defined as a place of paradox and interminable analysis.

Guillory himself—and here I part company with him—proposes a possible direction out of New Critical orthodoxy into a "state of heterodoxy where the *doxa* of literature is not a paralyzed allusion to a hidden god but a teaching that will enact discursively the struggle of difference" (359–60). But I see these brave words not as an effective replacement of the concealed religiosity of the old New Criticism, with its "hidden god," but as something closer to a new deconstructive mantra. In my view, the Yale version of deconstruction, especially as it was deployed by J. Hillis Miller and others, has led to yet another displacement of the transcendental, in which the concept of "difference" (or *differance*) itself becomes a universal signifier in a negative theology with a Calvinist coloration. This is especially apparent in a work like Miller's *The Ethics of Reading*, in which he argues that the reader of literature, doomed by *differance* to read wrongly, is nevertheless to be judged by the standard of an impossibly perfect reading. I have discussed this at some length elsewhere (Scholes, 1989) and will not repeat my arguments here. My point, however, is that the disciplinary shift from New Criticism to the American form of deconstruction should be seen as a still more desperate and constricted attempt to keep the transcendental aura of literature alive. Under this dispensation the great books are those that deconstruct themselves most fully, making the ethics of reading an act of endless expiation for an original sin of *differance,* from which no Redeemer will save us.

The deconstructive critics—and I would never deny the brilliance of the best of them—have been as alive as any of us to the problems caused for the field of literary study by the loss of Billy Phelps's easy connection between teaching and preaching. And they have helped to expose, as Guillory does so well, the "hidden god" behind the New Critical attempt to establish a purely literary value for literature. But the substitute that they have offered us has failed to answer to our needs and has even, along with other theoretical notions borrowed uncritically from analytic philosophy and neopragmatism, contributed both to our present problems and to the difficulty of finding a way out of them. I shall try to explain why, paying particular attention to neopragmatism, in Chapter 2. But first I must make my own theoretical position a bit clearer.

assignment 1

MY LIFE IN THEORY

A few years ago I was asked to write a short piece describing the relation between my commitments to literary theory and to the teaching of writing. The result was the following narrative, which has been slightly modified to fit in its present place.

Having been asked to be "timely" and to consider changes in my views over the past decade, I find that to be timely I need more time—going back to my beginnings in college. When I was admitted to Yale as an undergraduate (in 1946), prospective freshmen were asked to choose either of two English courses for their first year: English 10, a composition course, or English 15, an introduction to literature that featured Brooks and Warren's *Understanding Poetry*, along with Shakespeare and fiction. I chose the writing course without hesitation, because I thought at the time that I was destined to be a writer. My choice carried no weight, however, and I was put in a third course, English 25, a "masterpieces of English" course that was the gateway to the major in English literature. One thing leading to another, with a few deviations I have spent the rest of my life in "literature," but always with a rebellious "writer" inside me, making his presence known on various occasions.

In graduate school at Cornell in the late 1950s, my fellow student Larry Dembo made it clear to me that a career in English depended upon one's ability to publish literary criticism. This writing dimension of the profession appealed to me, but I quickly discovered that, though I had some gifts as a writer, I just didn't know how to produce the kind of writing that carried critical weight. Knowing what I know now, with the clarification of my thinking provided by Michel

Foucault in particular, I can see that my problem was a matter of gaining entry to a discourse that involved a certain cultural stance as well as specific rhetorical procedures. At the time, I sought blindly for models, first trying Edmund Wilson, who was not really academic enough, and then Lionel Trilling, whose lucid eloquence depended on greater learning and harder thinking than I could muster, and also upon membership in a certain New York City culture that gave his thought the stiffening and confidence that were so lacking in my own.

Fortunately, some of my teachers provided models closer to home, M. H. Abrams in particular, and W. R. Keast, who, along with his mentor R. S. Crane, who was visiting Cornell at that time, gave me some direct and necessary lessons in critical writing. Finally, near the end of my graduate career, I came upon the work of Erich Auerbach and Northrop Frye. Frye was such a powerful model that some of my early writing took the form of a clumsy pastiche of his work, verging on plagiarism in its happier moments. What I was learning from Auerbach at the same time was not a writing style but a way of analyzing prose passages that taught me something about styles in general as well as how to squeeze a short passage of text until it yielded plausible generalizations. At the same time, the amount of learning it took to write as these critics wrote was not lost upon me, and I knew only too well how far I was from that level of scholarly discipline. This left me with a severe sense of my limitations, so that I felt quite bashful about writing a critical dissertation and asked my advisers to help me find something humble and useful. The result was that they gave me the recently acquired papers of James Joyce to catalogue. This I did dutifully and with great pleasure, working two levels below ground, five days a week, from 9 to 5, for a whole year. The result was a dissertation with almost no writing in it at all—and certainly no theory or criticism.

I mention all this ancient history by way of showing that though I had been guided into the paths of literary study, I was thinking about writing all the time. I tried to write every oral report and term paper as if it were for publication, and ultimately a surprising amount of my apprentice work found its way into print. It was my orientation as a writer, I believe, that led me into literary theory. I always took a great interest in how effects were achieved, in how texts were constructed, and in how invisible generic structures exerted their power over the writer. As an undergraduate I had learned from a great art historian, George Kubler, something about the historical patterns of stylistic change in the visual arts. Auerbach, Abrams, Crane, and Frye directed my attention toward similar processes in verbal texts. The formal qualities of writing itself—all those elements of composition that are summed up in the notion of "style"—became a continuing source of interest to me.

There are two points about this history that I wish to emphasize. One is that I continued to write fiction and poetry while in graduate school, abandoning those ambitions slowly and with reluctance. Only my resolve to make writing important in my critical work enabled me to reconcile myself to this shift of energies. The other point is that my interest in theory and my interest in writing were aspects of the same concern for language and textual structures. This was why Northrop Frye was so important for a young scholar like myself. He was clearly a learned man, a theoretician, a sensitive reader, and yet his own prose was alive with energy, crackling with allusive wit: lucid, sinuous, and elegant. His range of interests extended well beyond belletristic prose. His search for a unified field theory of language, however flawed, however impossible in its goal, was an inspiration to me and many others of my generation.

It was the inspiration of Frye and Auerbach that led Robert Kellogg and me to attempt in the early 1960s a combined theory and history of Western narrative, but even this work had a base in the classroom, emerging directly from our experiences in devising a sophomore course at the University of Virginia. The book we produced, *The Nature of Narrative,* attracted the attention of a young structuralist theoretician, Tzvetan Todorov, who invited me, in the late sixties, to a conference on the semiotics of narrative in Urbino, Italy. From here, one thing led to another. The structuralists who interested me at that time—Todorov, Greimas, Genette among them —were all committed to the study of grammar, syntax, and rhetoric, both traditional and modern. To understand their work and to contribute to their ongoing discussions meant studying the linguistics of Saussure and the blend of linguistics, poetics, and rhetoric so powerfully deployed by Roman Jakobson. All the materials for a pedagogy that connected literary theory to the practice of writing were here, but by and large, the Europeans were far less interested in pedagogy than we North Americans were. For me, it took six years at the University of Iowa to bring pedagogical matters to the foreground of my attention.

In the late sixties—a time that forced many of us to examine the roots of our professional lives—I found that my last line of defense for my life as an English professor was that I taught reading and writing. At that time, I first saw clearly that English teachers from kindergarten to graduate school were engaged in the same process of helping students learn how to understand texts more fully and to express themselves more eloquently. I was fortunate, at Iowa, in working with people for whom teaching—and the teaching of writing in particular—was a central professional focus. I think in particular of Jix Lloyd-Jones and Carl Klaus, an old friend from graduate school. In addition to the usual literature courses, I got to devise my own courses in advanced composition (including one called Histor and Rhetor in which all the reading came from ancient historians, plus Aristotle's *Rhetoric*) and to work with Lloyd-Jones as he developed a remarkable team-taught course for undergraduates called English Semester, in which literary history was taught with an internal writing component.

In English Semester a group of twenty-five or thirty students registered for four courses and met with a team of three instructors for two hours a day, five days a week. We read English literature from the Renaissance through the nineteenth century, and students performed bits of plays in class and wrote regularly, imitating styles of various works in prose and verse and producing interpretive essays as well. In many ways these courses (which I taught for several years) were the most successful pedagogical effort I have ever undertaken. Participants emerged with a more genuine sense of the literary history of England than most students manage to acquire from any standard set of courses for a major in English. Still, the result left me feeling a bit hollow, especially in the light of what was going on around us in the late sixties. It all seemed too belletristic, too luxurious, too disconnected from other aspects of the lives of the students who had done so well and learned so much in the course. I could not imagine the job being done better, but I wondered whether it was quite the right job to be doing. From this point I date my sense that a major task for critical theory would be to rethink curricular and pedagogical practice.

Moving to Brown in the 1970s, I found my first chance for experiment coming from an offer by Andries Van Dam of the computer science faculty to devise a humanities course that could engage the capacities of a new system that he was working on, called Hypertext. Thinking the matter over, I came to the conclusion that the most hypertextual items in the English curriculum were poems. Working with two graduate students, Nancy R. Comley and James Catano, I tried to devise a syllabus that would use the ability of the system to display items from different parts of the database simultaneously. The details have been published by Catano. For our purposes here, the most important result was that students using the system wrote an average of eighty typed pages (or the equivalent) during the semester—and their writing improved, without any specific attention to their prose by the instructors. The system, which ultimately made all communications available to all participants, encouraged formal and informal exchanges among students as well as between students and instructors. With peer support—and peer pressure—writing about poetry, imitating poetic forms, and thinking about language had generated results that we long for in composition courses but too infrequently achieve.

Like the English semester experience at Iowa, the Hypertext experience at Brown contributed to my thinking about curricular and pedagogical matters. A challenge from a publisher to put our theories on the practical line led Comley and me to produce *The Practice of Writing*, a composition text using literary materials not as precious objects for exegesis but as samples of effective writing to be imitated, parodied, and responded to in other ways. The theoretical basis for this effort was a Jakobsonian sense that literary language differs from ordinary language not absolutely but only by different emphases. This also confirmed (and I think I can speak for Nancy Comley as well as myself in this) our sense that the most precious resource English departments have is a body of texts that embody the expressive possibilities of the English language.

At this point I began to understand that we make a mistake in thinking that we in English departments are properly responsible for all the possible kinds of writing in English. What we can teach about writing involves mainly those elements of it that are literary or rhetorical. Members of other faculties send us their students not so that we will teach them to write like social scientists or engineers but precisely so that we will teach them how to achieve the grace, clarity, and energy that we admire in literary texts. I remember discussing these matters with Kurt Vonnegut one evening in New York. He reached into his bookshelves and handed me a textbook with an inscription to him by one of the editors, Walter J. Miller. In that volume, which I borrowed, I found, among other things, an interview with Othmar H. Ammann.

Miller and his fellow editor had included in their book Ammann's proposal to build what became the George Washington Bridge over the Hudson River. In the interview Ammann said two striking things:

first, "most engineers think in terms of details. And so most engineering reports are cluttered with meaningless particulars"; and second, explaining how he had trained himself to write clear and vivid reports, "I rely on my studies of logic and literature. Logic taught me how to structure my writing. Literature gives me an understanding of the importance of style" (Miller and Saidla, 252). Throughout this exemplary textbook the editors focus on the "literary problems" faced by each writer in writing a particular response to a given situation, and the "literary techniques and devices" used to solve those problems. And the texts they offer include a number of translations from ancient engineers as well as the work of contemporaries like Ammann. Even this textbook for engineers, I found, stressed the "literary" side of writing. But what did the editors—or someone like Ammann—mean by *literary?*

I was still brooding about the various notions of *literature* active in our culture when I was asked to serve on the Modern Language Association's Commission on Writing and Literature. My several years of work on this Commission had a radicalizing effect on my thought. The Commission was charged with exploring ways of reconciling the split between composition and literature in the profession. What it discovered—or, at any rate, what I discovered while serving on it—was that the culture of English departments was structured by an invidious binary opposition between writing teachers and literary scholars that could not be improved by tinkering. Because the profession was organized by—indeed, founded upon—this distinction, it could be undone only by a deconstructive process striking at its roots. Let me try to make this more explicit. What I finally realized was that English departments need composition as the "other" of literature in order to function as they have functioned. The useful, the practical, and even the intelligible were relegated to composition so that literature could stand as the complex embodiment of cultural ideals, based upon texts in which those ideals were so deeply embedded as to require the deep analyses of a trained scholar. Teachers of literature became the priests and theologians of English, while teachers of composition were the nuns, barred from the priesthood, doing the shitwork of the field. This structure could be undone only by an assault on the notion of literature upon which it was founded.

What I could do about this, apart from the work of the Commission itself, was to use what I had learned from structuralist and poststructuralist theory to perform a deconstructive critique of the curriculum and pedagogy that embody the culture of "English." This effort, first deployed in *Textual Power* and put into practical form in *Text Book,* is still my concern. Among other things, I want to make a case for the importance of literariness—and the usefulness of many texts we call literary—precisely by denying the special mystical privileges we have accorded to "literature." To accomplish this I am using the resources of critical theory not only to deconstruct our traditional organization but to reconstruct our efforts as students and teachers of English around the notion of textuality. Under this sign, there is no difference between the theory of composition and the theory of literature—and there is precious little difference between theory and teaching at all, since the practice of teaching is based upon the teaching of theory, and this theory itself rests upon the shared stance of students and teachers as practitioners of reading and writing—textuality.

CHAPTER TWO

"No dog would go on living like this"

I would like to begin by putting before you statements on the topic of this chapter by two Victorian sages, whom I shall name in due course:

(1) Five great intellectual professions, relating to the daily necessities of life, have hitherto existed—three exist necessarily, in every civilized nation:
The Soldier's profession is to *defend* it.
The Pastor's to *teach* it.
The Physician's to *keep it in health*.
The Lawyer's to *enforce justice* in it.
The Merchant's is to *provide* for it.
And the duty of all these men is, on due occasion, to *die* for it.
    "On due occasion," namely:—
The Soldier, rather than leave his post.
The Physician, rather than leave his post in plague.
The Pastor, rather than teach Falsehood. . . .
                    [emphasis in original]

(2) But if this is how things stand in our time, then the dignity of philosophy is trampled into the dust; it has even become something ludicrous, it would seem, or a matter of complete indifference to anyone: so that it is the duty of all its true friends to bear witness against this confusion, and at the least to show that it is only its false and unworthy servants who are ludicrous or a matter of indifference. It would be

better still if they demonstrated by their deeds that *love of truth* is something fearsome and mighty. [emphasis added]

These words from the 1860s and 1870s ring strangely in our ears, to be sure. But I want to suggest that we attend to them nonetheless—at least as a way of situating ourselves. The first quotation comes from John Ruskin's series of lectures *Unto This Last.* He was addressing an audience of merchants, whom he hoped to enlist in the cause of social justice, hence his elevation of their work to the level of "intellectual profession." He introduced the military, this reader suspects, as a way of raising the stakes to the level of life and death, having observed that, although we may think that soldiers are hired to kill for their country, they are actually paid and respected because they are hired to die for it if necessary. But the other three professions—Law, Medicine, and Theology—are those included as the three higher faculties in Immanuel Kant's seminal essay of 1798, "The Conflict of Faculties." That essay, as Richard Rand has observed, became a "blueprint" for Wilhelm von Humboldt in founding the University of Berlin in 1810, thereby achieving "a success so canonical that, when American universities adopted it at the end of the [nineteenth] century, . . . a subtle and intricate invention had turned, so to speak, into a self-evident machine somewhat unmindful of its own inaugural circumstances" (Rand, vii–viii). That is—and I must emphasize this—our present university structures, down to the stripes that we wear on our academic robes, can be traced back to Kant's division of the faculties. (Kant's categories, of course, have their roots in medieval universities, but his systematization of them is the direct ancestor of our own usage.)

Ruskin, of course, by using the term *pastor,* has blurred the distinction between teaching and theology, and he has not included among his necessary professions those of the philosophers or scientists who, for Kant, constituted the lower faculty, bearing the title of Doctor of Philosophy: Ph.D. I keep mentioning Kant's essay because our attention has been drawn to it recently by two powerful—and very different—texts that treat of the present situation of university faculties: Pierre Bourdieu's sociological study of the French professoriat, *Homo Academicus* (see especially 62–63), and Jacques Derrida's lecture celebrating the centenary of the Columbia University Graduate School, "Mochlos; or the Conflict of Faculties."

Ruskin's point, insofar as it may be applied to teaching in general, is that the dignity of the profession depends upon its practitioners' reluctance to "teach Falsehood." Let me say unequivocally here that I stand with him on this question. Or, to put it more strongly, I believe that, if we teachers of the humanities cannot claim what my other Victorian sage called "the love of truth" as a part of our enterprise, that enterprise is in serious trouble. To sharpen the focus a bit, I believe that we are in trouble precisely because we have allowed ourselves to be persuaded that we cannot make truth claims but must go on "professing" just the same. Are we in trouble? Am I exaggerating our problems? Perhaps. But, at the very least, I think that many of us share in the feelings Derrida expressed in that lecture at Columbia, speaking as an academic to other academics: "We feel bad about ourselves. Who would dare to say otherwise? And those who feel good about themselves are perhaps hiding something, from others or from themselves" (Derrida, 1992, 7). There are many and good reasons why we professors in the humanities may feel bad about ourselves at the present time, but I believe that one of these reasons—in my judgment the crucial one—is that we have become reluctant to make claims of truth about the matters we teach. Powerful voices in our field have taught us to be embarrassed by the word *truth,* and thus either to avoid it or condemn it. These voices range from J. Hillis Miller and those I have called Yale deconstructionists to Richard Rorty, Stanley Fish, and other neopragmatists. I should add that many American students and teachers of literature believe they have learned something of the sort from Derrida, as well, but this, as I shall indicate later, is a questionable assumption. My undertaking, I must grant at the outset, reeks of the quixotic. Either truth needs no defense or its defense is impossible. Yet the idea of truth has been under attack for some time, both by philosophers like Rorty and by deconstructive literary critics, often drawing upon Nietzsche for support. What can be attacked can also be defended, even though the defense may be inadequate, and I must acknowledge some trepidation at trying to meet a trained philosopher and eloquent writer like Richard Rorty on his own ground. But I am heartened in this quixotic enterprise by two thoughts: one is that I shall be in some good company—I think of Umberto Eco and Christopher Norris first of all—and the other is that I shall draw considerable aid and comfort from the writing of Derrida himself, as well as from writers and thinkers often associated with him, including his well-known opponent, John R. Searle. And finally, I am emboldened by the fact that I am addressing the matter Professor Derrida put his finger on so acutely in his Columbia lecture—that "we feel bad about ourselves"—and that I am speaking out of my own heart and mind the truth as I understand it, that I am, in a use of the word now almost lost to us, professing.

My second epigraph is taken from the writing of another Victorian sage, who, like Ruskin, spent the last decade of his life and his century being cared for as an insane person: Friedrich Nietzsche. These words constitute the penultimate paragraph (1983, 194) of his youthful (1874) essay on "Schopenhauer as Educator," which is studded with praises of truthfulness and diagnoses of why the thinkers and teachers of his own time felt bad about themselves: "A certain gloominess and torpor lies upon even the finest personalities of our time, a feeling of ill-humor at the everlasting struggle between dissimulation and honesty which is being fought out within them, a lack of steady confidence in themselves—whereby they become quite incapable of being signposts and at the same time taskmasters for others" (133). It is true, of course, that Nietzsche contrasted Schopenhauer favorably in this essay with Kant, situating Schopenhauer as one whose truth led him out of the university while Kant clung to it, "submitted himself to regulations, retained the appearance of religious belief, endured to live among colleagues and students: so it is natural that his example has produced above all university professors and professorial philosophy" (137). The contempt attached by Nietzsche, young and old, to "university professors and professorial philosophy" should need no gloss here.

We who endure "to live among colleagues and students" are the sort of compromisers Nietzsche was coming to despise as his own academic career soured. But to understand his point here, we must rethink our notion of Kant, which is rather different from his. We have been taught to think of Kant as committed to a logocentric metaphysical project grounded in transcendental truths which we ought not to accept. But Nietzsche thought of Kant not just as an academic dissimulator but as an enemy of truth. In his essay on Schopenhauer, Nietzsche quotes approvingly the following passage from a letter of Heinrich von Kleist to his friend Wilhelmine von Zenge, written in 1801:

> Not long ago . . . I became acquainted with the Kantian philosophy—and now I have to tell you of a thought I derived from it, which I feel free to do because I have no reason to fear it will shatter you so profoundly and painfully as it has me.—We are unable to decide whether that which we call truth really is truth, or whether it only appears to us to be. If the latter, then the truth we assemble here is nothing after our death, and all our endeavour to acquire a possession which will follow us to the grave is in vain.— If the point of this thought does not penetrate your

heart, do not smile at one who feels wounded by it in
the deepest and most sacred part of his being. My one
great aim has failed me and I have no other. (140–41)

Nietzsche goes on to praise Schopenhauer as one who can lead
those who follow him away from the depths of Kantian "skeptical
gloom or criticizing renunciation" to new heights of tragic contemplation. He changed his view of Schopenhauer somewhat as he aged,
as he changed his view of his other early hero, Richard Wagner, and
he proceeded to argue that joy and affirmation lay on the other side of
those heights of tragic contemplation, where the overman might be
conceived. We may not wish to follow him on the road to the overman, but let us listen to him again before parting company with him:

Now, how does the philosopher view the culture of
our time? Very differently, to be sure, from how it is
viewed by those professors of philosophy who are so
well contented with their new state [the Bismarckian
Reich of 1871]. When he thinks of the haste and
hurry now universal, of the increasing velocity of life,
of the cessation of all contemplativeness and simplicity, he almost thinks that what he is seeing are the
symptoms of a total extermination and uprooting of
culture. The waters of religion are ebbing away and
leaving behind swamps or stagnant pools; the nations
are again drawing away from one another in the most
hostile fashion and long to tear one another to pieces.
The sciences, pursued without any restraint and in a
spirit of *laissez faire,* are shattering and dissolving all
firmly held belief; the educated classes and states are
being swept along by a hugely contemptible money
economy. . . . Everything, contemporary art and science included, serves the coming barbarism. (148)

Some of the conditions noted by Nietzsche's "philosopher" a hundred and twenty years ago have changed—though not necessarily for the better—and others have persisted. But my main reason for citing him at such length is to remind you that the Nietzsche so often presented to us today as the great destroyer of concepts of truth and morality is based on a very selective reading of his work that ignores what Karen Carr has recently called "his constant appeal to health and sickness, strength and weakness, as criteria" (K. Carr, 50), to which I would add his indispensable and perpetual distinction between high and low, often to be read as a contrast between high culture and the culture of the "herd" that he despised. One of the things that has not changed—or changed in only a superficial way— is that skepticism about the possibilities of truth, whether Kantian or Rortian, still haunts academic humanists, who find themselves in a situation that is well described, once again, by Nietzsche himself:

> Here and there a man is equipped by nature with mental acuteness, his thoughts like to do the dialectical two-step; how easy it is, if he carelessly lets go the reins of his talent, for him to perish as a human being and to lead a ghostly life in almost nothing but "pure knowledge"; or, grown accustomed to seeking the for and against in all things, for him to lose sight of truth altogether and then be obliged to live without courage or trust, in denial and doubt, agitated and discontented, half hopeful, expecting to be disappointed: "No dog would go on living like this!" (144, translation slightly modified)

The passage closes with a quotation from Goethe, in which Faust expresses his loathing for the academic life that has brought him respect ("Master and Doctor are my titles"), and condemns himself for holding "erudite recitals" and leading his pupils "by the nose" while "knowing the emptiness of what I teach" (part I, scene i). Faust is, in Derrida's phrase, an academic who feels bad about himself—a feeling that leads him to abandon philosophy for magic and the devilish satisfactions that it offers. Which brings us back to ourselves, for it is we who feel bad about ourselves and might accept a devilish bargain if only Mephistopheles would appear and make us an offer. But perhaps we feel bad because he has already appeared and we have accepted his offer. (I speak metaphorically or allegorically, of course.)

Let me put things in more concrete terms. I think we feel bad because we do not believe in the significance of the research that is required of us—for the Ph.D. itself and for professional progress afterward—and because we are confused about what we should be teaching, and how, and why. Listen to the way Derrida posed these questions at the beginning of his Columbia lecture:

> If we could say *we* (but have I not already said it?), we might perhaps ask ourselves: where are we? And who are we in the university where apparently we are? *What* do we represent? *Whom* do we represent? Are we responsible? For what and to whom? If there is a university responsibility, it at least begins with the moment when a need to hear these questions, to take them upon oneself and respond, is imposed. This imperative for responding is the initial form and minimal requirement of responsibility. (1992, 3)

Derrida's lecture proceeds to focus on the question of "university responsibility" by situating Kant's *Conflict of Faculties* as a founding document and proceeding, elegantly, to deconstruct it, revealing the conflicts within Kant's own thinking that make his university, however practical he intended his conception to be, an impossible object. Yet this impossible object was created and emulated, in all its impossibilities, to such an extent that we still inhabit it, though the world has changed so much as to make the conflicts and impossibilities in the situation of universities much more acute. Now, says Derrida, we "live in a world where the formation of a new law—in particular a new university law—is necessary" (30). The lecturer's hour is late, however, the university is closing up, so there is no time for Derrida to make any specific recommendations about this new law, only the observation that such a new dispensation is already on the way, and the hope that it will take shape as the result of a dialectical process involving the inside and the outside, the doctors of philosophy and the more worldly doctors of law and medicine, the faculty and the government, the left and the right. An acute mind, doing what Nietzsche called the "dialectical two-step" *(dialektischen Doppelgang)*. An elegant essay, but not much help in figuring out what "we" should do next.

The other essays collected after Derrida's in Richard Rand's *Logomachia* share some of his brilliance—and most of his evasiveness. We never find what Derrida's opening words encouraged us to expect: a clear answer to the question posed about the nature of university responsibility. But on some occasions the difficulties that we face are put with all the specificity one could wish, as when Robert Young discusses the problems faced by literary theorists in the English universities when the Thatcher government decided to cut their subsidies:

> The difficulty for literary theorists, when faced with a new "technologico-Thatcherite" assault on the humanities, was that the terms by which their subject was established historically, and the only effective terms with which it could still be defended, were those of the cultural conservatism and humanist belief in literature and philosophy that "literary theory" has, broadly speaking, been attacking since the 1970s. When theorists found themselves wanting to defend their discipline against successive government cuts they discovered that the only view with which they

could vindicate themselves was the very one which, in intellectual terms, they wanted to attack. (113)

In "Mochlos" Derrida points out that Kant's division of faculties — into the higher, more worldly departments that necessarily spoke for and answered to the government, and the lower, philosophical faculty engaged in pure thought — was an impossible division from the beginning. And Derrida's recommendation for the present, to the extent that his cryptic conclusions can be put in such a straightforward form, is that we of the "lower" faculty must accept the impurity of our situation and work both with and against our more worldly brethren. Derrida, like Kant, works in an institution finally answerable to his nation itself, whereas most of us in the United States work for institutions answerable either to the governments of particular states or to trustees who represent, for the most part, corporate wealth. Let me explore the implications of this situation for a moment.

In the present division of faculties in American universities, the rise of applied sciences has added to the size and power of the "higher" or more worldly side of the division. Technological truth, if I may apply that term to applications of science that yield results in economic or military terms, is highly cherished in a social framework that is both capitalistic and (though perhaps clumsily) imperialistic as well. Thus the faculties that offer technological truth in the form of engineering, computer science, biotechnology, and applications of physics and chemistry — these faculties that have taken their places alongside law and medicine — have, in fact, replaced the faculty of theology, which in our mainly secular institutions has become just another humanity, if it exists at all. And the humanities, as we now call Kant's philosophical faculty (including philosophy itself as a small department within the larger division), having largely given up on the search for pure truth that once justified their special status, are finding it difficult to compete within the university structure in terms of faculty positions, salaries, and support for research. (It is worth noting, by the way, that the status of the humanities continues to sink just at the moment when they are moving toward a gender balance in their faculties, while the "higher" faculties continue to be dominated by men.) We in the humanities are also finding it difficult, for the reasons mentioned by Robert Young with respect to Oxford and Cambridge, to explain to the public and to our trustees just what it is that we do—and we are finding it even harder to justify our doing it, especially if we tell the truth about what we are doing.

The truth about what we are doing is not pretty. The spate of recent attacks on universities, and especially on their humanities faculties, has been both dangerous and infuriating. These books and essays offend us partly because they are full of distortions if not outright lies. But they also worry us because even the worst of them often catches some glimpse of a troubling reality. Our system of rewarding published research was originally grounded on the belief in a search for truth that would be progressive. Johns Hopkins, the first modern American university founded explicitly on the German model—which Harvard and other schools quickly emulated—has for its motto, *Veritas Vos Liberavit,* the Truth Shall Make You Free. The sciences still work on this model, assuming that the publication of research will lead progressively toward true knowledge—and, not incidentally, to technological truths with economic and military implications. Their truth may make you rich as well. But in the humanities we have largely given up on research as a progress toward truth—though we have not fully realized the implications of having done so.

Why have we done this? Nietzsche believed that academic doctors of philosophy were cut off from the truth because of their necessary subservience to the state that employed them—a subservience of which they might not even be fully aware. But that is not our situation. We seldom think of any responsibility we might have to our trustees or legislators, and we have enjoyed an astonishing autonomy, despite the occasional witch hunt, for some decades. Even attacks from the political right wing in recent years have made little impact on what we do. Economic pressures might be changing our working conditions for the worse, but that worse shows no signs of taking the form of orders to teach this or that text in this or that way. Many college and university teachers of language and literature would be embarrassed if they had to explain to their legislature or trustees exactly what methods of reading, or ideological positions, they are advocating in class. Our masters seem either not to know or not to care just what we are doing, or perhaps they do not really feel like our masters. Having no more truth than we do, having only their own devotion to the morality of the marketplace and the aesthetics of fashion, they may feel in no great position to tell us what to do.

We, too, of course, are driven to an extraordinary extent by these two forces—fashion and the marketplace. We live in an academic world in which we are rewarded not so much according to how well we teach or how much we learn but by the amount we publish and the attention it attracts from others. Instead of the search for truth, what we have is a conversation in which the rewards go to the best conversationalists. Richard Rorty and Stanley Fish, I believe, would be quick to point out that there is nothing wrong with this situation and a good deal that is right. I would like to acknowledge the strength of their position—not to mention the conversational strength and skill with which they both present it. Yet at the same time I want to argue that we must reject it, because it rationalizes and endorses the very situation that is at the root of our feeling bad about ourselves: our estrangement from the possibility of truth. Rorty's position— and some of its problems—emerge clearly in his reply (using Donald Davidson as a screen for his own views) to a statement that I made at a conference a few years ago:

> Davidson can happily agree with the claim (made in Scholes's "Foreword") that "some descriptions of things are better or worse than others, more or less

accurate, more or less fair, more or less comprehensive, more or less clear." But he will insist that adjectives like *"accurate," "better," "clear," "true,"* and so on have nothing to do with a relation between descriptions and things-as-they-are-under-no-description. They are, rather, ways of describing the relation between a description and the rest of the human practices within which the use of that description occurred. (Rorty, 1993, 187, emphasis added)

In the published proceedings of that conference, Rorty had the last word, but this is my text, so things will be different here. To begin with, I want to quote a slightly fuller version of the passage (from my foreword, referring somewhat confusingly to my afterword) to which he was responding:

My Afterword is in fact an acknowledgment that I got something wrong that I must now attempt to set right. This concern about getting things "right" is an essential aspect of our academic discourse, without which we could not operate as we do. I see no reason why we should avoid thinking of it as a concern for "truth," nor do I see how our study and teaching could continue without the fundamental assumption that some descriptions of things are better or worse than others, more or less *accurate,* more or less *fair,* more or less *comprehensive,* more or less *clear.* How could we do without judgments of this kind? If we do not wish to call these protocols of our discourse a concern for truth, then we had better find some other name for them rather than pretend that we have no such concerns at all. For to deny such concerns would eliminate our very reasons for being and doing what we do and the rationale for the institutions that sustain us in those endeavors. (Scholes, 1993, 169–70, emphasis added)

We can learn something about Rorty's values and his methods by attending closely to what he has done with the evaluative terms I proposed as specifications of the loose and general notions of better and worse. The terms Rorty attributes to me in quotation marks are *accurate, better, clear,* and *true.* The evaluative terms I actually used were *accurate, fair, comprehensive,* and *clear.* What Rorty has done is to avoid some of those terms that involve comparison between a description and its object. Fair is fair only by our standards, to be sure, but we cannot say whether something is fairly represented—even by our standards—without some inspection of the thing itself. *Comprehensive* must mean comprehensive in relation to our standards of comprehensiveness, of course, but it also involves a judgment about the relation between any description and the thing described. I am not talking about something metaphysical here, what Rorty calls "things-as-they-are-under-no-description," which he sometimes equates with the Kantian thing-in-itself. I am talking about a particular thing that might be described in different ways, more or less fairly, more or less comprehensively, more or less accurately: a thing such as the passage from my foreword which Rorty has described for us. And I am saying that, in selecting the terms that he would list, Rorty left himself open to criticism on precisely the grounds of fairness and comprehensiveness—the concepts that he elected to suppress in making his list. That is, to the extent that Rorty's words are a description of my words, it is possible to inspect both sets of words and to evaluate the accuracy of his description. Neither of these sets of words is more or less of a thing-as-it-is-under-no-description than the other, but they stand in a relation of descriptive text and described text which can only be evaluated by comparison. An evaluation of Rorty's description made only in terms of "the rest of the human practices within which the use of that description occurred," and without an actual comparison between the two texts, would be absurd.

There is a philosophical issue here, which no mere literary scholar can expect to influence. It is, however, an issue still seriously disputed in philosophy, though many literary critics seem to believe that it has been settled. The chapters called "Does the Real World Exist?" and "Truth and Correspondence" in John R. Searle's recent book, *The Construction of Social Reality,* make a strong argument on behalf of our ordinary usage of words like *fact* and *truth,* while also defending philosophical realism and the correspondence theory of truth. I take comfort from Searle's view, which, as I have said, indicates that the issue is far from settled among serious philosophers. But there is also a less philosophical argument to be made about verbal texts constructed by human beings, which is that such texts do not exist "under no description," since they come to us already inscribed in a language that constrains the ways we may respond to them. My original words, Rorty's reading of those words, and my reading of his words—all exist on the same plane, as textual objects partly self-described, and equally available for inspection.

Perhaps I am wrong. Perhaps my description of Rorty's description is itself unfair, inaccurate, not comprehensive enough. So be it, but we will never get anywhere if we insist that one or both of these textual objects must be inaccessible for purposes of comparison. Rorty has said that he has no objections to the word *truth*— and that he wants to assert the truth of his own neopragmatist views. But what he means by *true* is, as he says, using William James as his screen, "what is good for *us* to believe" (Rorty, 1991, vol. 1, 22, emphasis in original). This is a view that he has repeated on many occasions and in many variations, but its problems are the same in all its variants. Two of them lie in the difficulty—if not the impossibility—of defining *good* and *us* in satisfactory ways. Rorty's *us*—and it is the word that does the most work in his later philosophy—is an extremely slippery category, sometimes meaning everyone in the "rich North-Atlantic liberal democracies," and sometimes only philosophical neopragmatists like himself. The word, as Derrida has often pointed out, cannot be used rigorously. *Good* is at least as difficult a concept as *truth,* with meanings ranging from "comforting in the short run" to "leading to desirable results in the long run." Taken in either sense, I do not believe that it is good for professors of the humanities to abandon the "love of truth" that Nietzsche considered so essential for philosophy.

Moreover, even if we try to accept Rorty's notion of truth as simply what it is good for *us* to believe, other problems arise. For instance, if we truly saw everything only in terms of our existing beliefs and practices, we would never find any reason to change those beliefs and practices. That is, we could never understand or consider seriously anything that did not "fit" with what we already knew. The path from the Enlightenment to ourselves begins when appeals can be made from belief to experiment, from dogma to nature. And Rorty likes where we are. He feels that the Enlightenment is justified precisely because it led to *us* and to *our* institutions. Without stopping to challenge this debatable point (in which I might find myself partly on Rorty's side), I want simply to note that this means that Rorty is urging us to enjoy the fruits of the Enlightenment while chopping down the tree itself, root and branch.

This problem in Rorty's position is not simply an academic one but a matter of our social and political life as a whole. And the problem repeats itself at the level of the university and its practices. In this respect I want to cite the cogent critique made of Rorty and Stanley Fish recently by Jonathan Culler. Culler puts it this way:

> What I have always found particularly disquieting about contemporary American Pragmatism—of Rorty and Fish, for example—is that people who attained their positions of professional eminence by en-

gaging in spirited debate with other members of the
academic field, such as philosophy or literary studies,
by identifying the difficulties and inconsistencies of
their elders' conceptions of the field and by proposing
alternative procedures and goals, have, once they have
attained professional eminence, suddenly turned and
rejected the idea of a system of procedures and body
of knowledge where argument is possible and presented the field as simply a group of people reading books and trying to say interesting things about
them. They thus seek systematically to destroy the
structure through which they attained their positions
and which would enable others to challenge them in
their turn. (1992, 118)

Though I agree with what Culler is saying here, I cannot resist pointing out that his criticism of neopragmatism is made less clearly than
it might have been because he, too, is concerned to avoid the em-
barrassing T-word: truth. In his insistence that we professors need
a "system of procedures and body of knowledge where argument is
possible," he is right on the mark. But beyond that, the charge Culler
makes against Rorty and Fish within the academy is equally valid
with respect to Rorty's position on our social and political structure
itself. If there is no appeal to realities or principles beyond what we
may happen to believe at any given time, then we have no arguments either in favor of changing things for the better or for resisting
a slide back into superstition and dogma. And we live in a world
where we are threatened by superstition and dogma at every turn.
On very pragmatic grounds, then, I would want to argue in favor of
what Rorty calls a realistic position, as opposed to a pragmatic one,
because it is "good for *us* to believe." Quite specifically, it is good for
us to believe that our beliefs are grounded in something firmer than
belief itself. We need the love of truth, not because we can attain

ultimate truth, nor yet because it will "make us free"—but for the reasons touched on by Kleist in his letter to Wilhelmine von Zenge. That is, we need the sense of a shared enterprise, to which we may contribute something. As educators, we need the sense that we are presenting to students and colleagues ideas, methods, and information that are neither false nor useless. We need reasons for believing in our beliefs. We need protocols of reading and teaching.

I think Derrida, for instance, needs them, as is plain in this anguished response to a description of his work by Habermas:

> Although *I am not cited a single time,* although not one of my texts is even indicated as a reference in a chapter of twenty-five pages that claims to be a long critique of my work, phrases such as the following can be found: "Derrida is particularly interested in standing the primacy of logic over rhetoric, canonized since Aristotle, on its head" (p. 187), ". . . the deconstructionist can deal with the works of philosophy as works of literature . . ." (p. 188), ". . . in his business of deconstruction, Derrida does not proceed analytically. . . . Instead [he] proceeds by a critique of style . . ." (sic! p. 189). That is false. I say *false,* as opposed to *true,* and I defy Habermas to prove the presence in my work of that "primacy of rhetoric" which he attributes to me. (1988, 156–57, emphases in original)

In this instance, as in many others, Derrida invites us to compare a description of something (in this case his own writing) with the thing under description, just as if that thing under description were present to our inspection—or, at least sufficiently present to offer a check on the truth or falsehood of the description.

Even Rorty himself needs protocols of teaching, as, for instance, when he concludes his "Pragmatist's Progress" by insisting that if we try to "make an invidious distinction between getting it right and making it useful" we will "betray what Heidegger and Derrida were trying to tell us" (1992, 108). Let us pause and consider this phrase for a moment: "*betray* what Heidegger and Derrida were trying to *tell* us." *Tell* in this instance is a euphemism for *teach.* That is, Rorty is talking about what he takes to be the teaching of Heidegger and Derrida, which we will *betray* if we persist in our wish to make a distinction between getting it right and making it useful. Now it was useful to Habermas, presumably, to describe Derrida's teaching in a manner that Derrida called "false as opposed to true." And useful to Derrida, presumably, to call this description false. But what will it be useful to *us* to think about this dispute? Quite simply, what will be most useful to us will be to get it right, according to the protocols of our scholarship, which will have to include some comparison of the description to the thing described, raising such questions as, "Is this description accurate? Is it fair? Is it comprehensive?"

In Rorty's wish to prevent us from betraying the teachings of Heidegger and Derrida, a number of concerns are betrayed, especially in that word: *betray.* What would it mean to *betray* the teachings of Heidegger and Derrida? Would it mean to misunderstand them—or to regard them as false—or simply to consider them not useful? The word *betray* betrays Rorty's own commitment to getting Heidegger and Derrida right (while arguing that J. Hillis Miller has got them wrong!), but I would insist that, in this case, he gets Derrida wrong himself—and in much the same way that Habermas got Derrida wrong. My point is simply that not even Rorty himself can function according to his own protocols. He wants to get Heidegger and Derrida right and not simply to use them for his own purposes. And I honor him for this wish, which runs counter to his own explicit position. This honorable inconsistency is one reason for rejecting his views. There is also, however, a more properly "pragmatic" reason. His proposal that we consider as true whatever is good for *us* to believe turns out to be bad for *us* to believe, not simply because it is useless when we need it most, but because it puts us in a situation that "no dog" would continue to accept.

Rorty's overt position, as opposed to the covert one betrayed by his commitment to getting Heidegger and Derrida right, is quite different from that adopted recently by Stanley Fish in his Clarendon Lectures, published as *Professional Correctness: Literary Studies and Political Change*. These lectures frame an argument against the use of English courses as a means toward political ends and against any shift from literary toward cultural studies. The focus of the argument is on the special status of literary interpretation as the disciplinary core of English. I shall address this issue briefly in the concluding pages of my last chapter, but at this point I must note that, in making his argument, Fish is led to base his notion of literary interpretation on nothing other than the love of truth. *Mirabile dictu!* as my old Latin teacher, Miss Jennings, used to remark when I turned in my homework on time. But let us see what Fish says:

> Were I to offer a reading of *Paradise Lost,* it could be challenged at any point by someone who believed (and could back up his belief with discipline-specific reasons) that his reading was the better one. Each of us would be proceeding politically; but neither of us would be proceeding with a political intention because we would both be *possessed by the same desire, to get at the truth* about *Paradise Lost.* (Fish, 67, emphasis added)

In the preface to his book, where Fish is doing his best to control the way we interpret him, he tells his readers how to behave: "Do not read [this book] as evidence that I have changed my mind" (Fish, x). It would never have occurred to me that he might have changed his mind "yet once more" if he hadn't protested so much about it in his preface, but now I can't get it out of my head. Has he always considered the love of truth so important in interpretation? No matter—he is with me now, and I welcome his support, as I welcome Rorty's less voluntary confirmation of his commitment to truthfulness, and Derrida's attack on Habermas's failure to "get at the truth" (as Fish says) about his own work. Between a commitment to truthfulness and an acceptance of solipsism, there is very little room to maneuver.

If I have done my work well enough up to this point, my reader should now be wondering whether I have anything positive to offer. "So," you may be thinking, "Scholes says we feel bad about ourselves and that neopragmatism is part of the problem rather than a solution to the problem. If, for the sake of argument, I agree with some of what he has said, what has he got to offer teachers of the humanities beyond some nebulous notion of *truth?*" My notion of academic truth, I must respond, is not profound but neither is it nebulous. I have already touched upon it. It resides in words at a lower order of abstraction: words like *fair, accurate,* and *comprehensive.* In a discipline called English the minimal requirements for academic truth include scrupulous accuracy in citation, regard for what is already known about our subject, and rigor in situating and interrogating whatever material we are considering. These are necessary and fundamental. But there are also larger considerations.

The "love of truth" seems to me the first protocol of teaching, upon which any others that we might devise would depend. And I mean to include in this notion both the seeking of truth and a scrupulous truthfulness in our teaching, which includes the admission of the weak or dubious elements in what we profess. Truthfulness begins in a rigorous attention to the grounds of our own beliefs and a willingness to be corrected. As a habit of mind, the love of truth is one of the great things that we, as teachers, have to offer, but we cannot offer it by merely talking about it; we have to enact it, to embody it in our whole practice as scholars and teachers. This means being truthful with ourselves about how we came to be where we are, what interests we are serving, and what good we can hope to accomplish. It means ending what I will call (in the next chapter) hypocriticism, and taking a new approach to our culture, our textual canon, our curriculum, and our classroom practice. For English teachers it means reconsidering how we became what we are and what we do. And above all, it means trying to answer those questions posed by Jacques Derrida, questions so important that I must repeat them here:

> And who are we in the university where apparently we are? *What* do we represent? *Whom* do we represent? Are we responsible? For what and to whom? If there is a university responsibility, it at least begins with the moment when a need to hear these questions, to take them upon oneself and respond, is imposed. This imperative for responding is the initial form and minimal requirement of responsibility. (1992, 3)

I shall begin an attempt to answer Derrida's question, for myself and others like me, in Chapter 3, but first another look at the relation between teaching, learning, and truth.

assignment 2

THEORY IN THE CLASSROOM

David Laurence, director of the MLA's Association of Departments
of English, asked me to speak on the role of theory in the English
classroom to a group of faculty considering changes in their curriculum. The following lecture was my response to that assignment.
I have made some changes, especially in the concluding paragraphs,
to connect this discussion more directly to the argument of the
present book.

David Laurence has asked me to speak for twenty minutes about
how, "for better or for worse, critical and theoretical sophistication
affects the way faculty members observe students and respond to
what students do as readers and writers" (letter of 2 Dec. 1992). The
first thing I notice in David's letter is that echo of the marriage service from the Anglican *Book of Common Prayer*. And I imagine myself as having been wedded to Theory, some years ago, in a ceremony
which went, "I, Robert, take thee, Theory, to my wedded Wife, to
have and to hold from this day forward, for better for worse, for
richer for poorer . . . " and so on. Well, we have had our ups and
downs over the years, Theory and I, but we are still together. I can
certainly admit, however, that, as far as Theory is concerned, "age
cannot whither, nor custom stale, her infinite variety." And it is this
variety that constitutes my problem in generating an adequate response to David's invitation. Which theory is it to be—what kind of
critical sophistication—that I should assume as the perspective from
which to view the student and the classroom?

I can, for instance, imagine David Bleich observing and responding to his students. I can also imagine Jane Gallop, or Gayatri Spivak,

or E. D. Hirsch in the classroom. What I cannot imagine is a single theoretical perspective that would unite these professors' views of students or their classroom practice. Yet every one of them possesses (or is possessed by) theoretical sophistication. The "simple" solution would be to make a categorical imperative of my own theoretical position and assume that every right-thinking teacher will share it. My problem with this (and the reason for the scare quotes around *simple*) is that I am still trying to work out this position. All these years living with Theory, you may well say, and he still doesn't understand her. Well, yes. That is where I am. The trouble is, Theory keeps changing, and I keep changing. Instead of beginning then with My Theory, let me begin with two anecdotes of schooling—anecdotes about a famous theoretician in the classroom—not as teacher but as student.

The theoretician-as-student in question is Louis Althusser, who has given us a fascinating account of his student years in his autobiography, *L'avenir dure longtemps* (The future lasts a long time). The first anecdote concerns his days at the lycée Saint-Charles in Marseilles, when he was sixteen or seventeen years old. It was there that an admired teacher directed him away from the École Polytechnique, toward which he had been headed, and set him on his path to the École Normale Supérieure and his future as a philosopher. Of this teacher, M. Richard, Althusser writes, "He introduced us, and with what warmth, tenderness, and success! to the great writers and poets of history." And he continues: "I identified myself completely with him. . . . I readily imitated his writing, took up in succession his pet phrases, adopted his tastes, his judgments, even imitated his voice and tender inflections, and in my papers presented him with an exact image of himself. He quickly discerned my merits" (Althusser, 80, all translations from this book are mine). Pursuing a similar path of emulation with other teachers, Althusser was much admired and was expected to win prizes in national and regional examinations. But he failed miserably to finish anywhere near the top in those evaluations.

Reflecting on these experiences, he concludes that he had seduced his teachers "by imitation of their personalities and manners" so that "they recognized themselves so well in me that they had either projected on me the idea they had of themselves, or offered themselves unconsciously their own nostalgias and hopes. Whence my setbacks when I competed before judges that I had not had the opportunity of seducing! Then all my artifices, which were artifices *ad hominem* and worked only in the relationship of seduction . . . no longer worked but produced a fiasco" (82). This is mildly interesting, but in Althusser's autobiography it only serves as the prelude to an even more revealing episode of a similar sort. When his father was posted to a bank in Lyons, young Louis entered a lycée there (Lycée du Parc) for the final years of preparation for entrance to the École Normale Superieure. He was unhappy in his new school at first, both because he was new and not accepted by the other students and because his preparation for classes in philosophy had been inadequate. His teacher in this field, Jean Guitton, was demanding and intimidating. Given a "dissertation" to write on a subject he has since forgotten, Althusser indulged himself in what he calls "lyrical lamentations with neither reasoning nor rigor" (84). For this effusion he received a grade of 7 out of a possible 20 points and some marginal comments on the order of "not at all to the point."

This disaster was soon followed by a composition to be written in a large study hall, in which various classes were mixed. The subject assigned by Guitton was "the real and the fictional." Here is Althusser's description of what happened:

> I set myself vainly to drawing from my head a few vague notions, and I saw myself lost again when an older student approached me with some pages in his hand. "Here, take this, it could help you. Anyway, it's the same subject."
>
> In fact, Guitton must have set the same topic the

year before, and the veteran had offered me his own
paper with Guitton's corrections. I was thoroughly
ashamed, but my despair was stronger. Wasting no
time I took over the corrections of the teacher, keeping the essential things (the divisions, their themes,
and the conclusion), adapting them as best I could in
my own fashion—that is to say to what I had already
picked up of the manner of Guitton, a restrained
writer. When Guitton returned the papers in class, he
smothered me in sincere and astonished praise: how
could I have made such progress in such a short time!
I was first, with 17 out of 20. (84)

Well. Now we have before us an example of Theory in the
Classroom—or of the budding theoretician in the classroom—about
which we can theorize a bit. These were French classrooms, to be
sure, in the 1930s, but to assume that we have no lessons to learn
from these anecdotes would be a mistake. So let's look into them
a bit. First question: is this the same event repeating itself, or is
the second episode significantly different from the first? I believe, as
Althusser himself believed, that the second imposture was different
in a number of important respects from the first one. It is, to be
sure, another case of presenting a teacher with an image of himself
that he cannot help but admire. But it is not exactly the same kind
of image, nor was the teacher the same kind of teacher. In the first
case, what the boy took from his teachers and used to seduce them
were "pet phrases," "tastes," "judgments," "voice," and "inflections."
In the second case what he took were ideas and a restrained style of
expressing them. Still artifices, still tricks, to be sure, but more useful
ones because they would prove, in the long run, to be not "artifices
ad hominem" but tricks of the trade.

Althusser speaks eloquently of the guilt he felt at this "theft,"
which was so much more blatant and conscious than his previous

seduction of his teachers by imitating them. He felt, he tells us, not only that he did not exist in his own right, but that he was *"guilty of not existing"* (85). He also speaks frankly of what he had gained by it: acceptance by his schoolmates and the special attention of his teacher, a strong Christian, a disciple of Cardinal Newman, among others. This teacher, Jean Guitton, soon took the boy into his confidence, showed his work to his pupil, and even took him to Paris, where the young Louis Althusser delivered an address philosophically condemning materialism—before an audience of nuns. More important than these opportunities, however, in his own eyes, was that he learned from "this admirable pedagogue" who was not "a great philosopher"

> two virtues proper to the university, which later played a great part in my success: First, the most extreme clarity of writing, then, the art (still an artifice) of composing and writing on no matter what subject, a priori and as if by deduction from the void, a dissertation which would hold together and be convincing. That I succeeded as I did at the entrance exam for the École Normale and then at the final examination in philosophy, I owe entirely to him. Because he had given me (and without this I would have had to develop it laboriously) the knowledge not of arbitrary artifices, but of precisely those artifices that would enable me . . . to gain recognition in the university at the highest levels.
>
> It is clear that henceforth I conceived an idea of the university (as of myself) that was neither glorious nor respectful, which I have never lost, and which, rightly understood, has both helped and hindered me. (86)

Now we are in a position to theorize more fully about the experiences of this budding theoretician. Having learned a bad and debilitating set of tricks that enabled him to manipulate his teachers in Marseilles, he began, by an act that he does not hesitate to call theft, to learn a good and empowering set of tricks that would enable him to manipulate the entire French university system and to have a brilliant academic career, with an influence that has extended powerfully into American academic life as well. He learned that he was a fraud, and that the university system was a fraud—and that they were the same kind of fraud. (This is not the occasion to go into Althusser's personal life and its bitter end—his bouts of madness, his confinements in asylums or clinics, and the insane murder of his wife—except, perhaps, to note that he made these revelations only after those terrible events and his subsequent disgrace, when he had nothing to lose by making them, and perhaps something to gain.) As he describes from this distance his "fraudulent" academic successes, he tells us also that what he found out about the university was later extended to the nation as a site of power. There, too—and he credits Machiavelli with helping him understand this—there is a void, a fraudulent space in which artifice not only can but must work. He ultimately found in Marxism, of course, a ground upon which his artifice might rest, but, as he acknowledges in his autobiography, his is a Marxism that he constructed himself by ignoring the contradictions and the eschatological ambitions that he found in Marx's texts.

Let me now try to turn the lesson of Althusser into a form that may be relevant to our practice as teachers of English. We have a word for the artifices that Althusser employed in his youthful attempts at academic success. The word is *rhetoric*. He had bad teachers who allowed him to get by with learning a rhetoric that had no textual power beyond the domains of their own classrooms. And he had a good teacher who taught him a rhetoric that stood by him throughout his career as student, teacher, and political philosopher. We are used to the Platonic distinction between a *rhetoric* that is Sophistical and a *dialectic* that moves toward the true ideas of things—a distinction evoked by Habermas in his (sophistical) attack on Derrida as a rhetorician. But Althusser, like the other figures who have had the greatest influence on theory over the past few decades, rejects the possibility of any dialectical discourse leading to truth. What we can attempt to offer our students are the artifices that work, a rhetoric that will enable them to gain the respectful attention of those around them for their feelings, thoughts, and values.

It means also that we teachers must employ a pedagogical rhetoric that will earn for us the respectful attention of those we are teaching. To come back to Althusser, I like the image of him solemnly addressing an audience of nuns on the philosophical inadequacies of materialism, because I see this against his later admiration for that arch-materialist, Ludwig Feuerbach, and his career as an interpreter of Marx and Lenin. What we should notice here, however, is not merely this local or personal irony but the different results of his instruction in values and in methods. Most of his teachers, and the extracurricular groups that he joined while in school, were staunchly religious. In and out of class his instructors regularly attacked the twin specters of socialism and materialism, with the result that this future communist became interested in the object of these attacks. My point is that he did not absorb the values that even his best teachers would have liked to teach him. What he absorbed and retained was their good rhetorical habits, even as he ultimately rejected their values. To come back to our own situation, I think we may at present be too concerned with teaching the right ideas in the classroom and not concerned enough with teaching the most effective ways of speaking, listening, reading, and writing.

What I would advocate, as a theoretical way of looking at our students, is to start by thinking of what they need to know and what they need to be able to do, with respect to those things that are in our domain—and our domain is the domain of textuality. In constructing the syllabus for every class, as in the curriculum as a whole, we need to interrogate every text we select, and every bit of work we assign, with respect to how this will help our students toward the rhetorical abilities they need. How will knowing this or doing that strengthen them as thinkers, as readers, as communicators? The one thing a curriculum in English *must* do, whatever else it accomplishes on the way, is to lead students to a position of justified confidence in their own competence as textual consumers and their own eloquence as producers of texts. This also means, of course, that, along the way, we must be assigning the right texts and responding to the work of our students with an informed and rigorous sense of the rhetorical skills that they need to develop.

Much more could be said about these matters, and there are other aspects of those episodes in the life of Louis Althusser that might easily be discussed in this context. My main point in presenting them, though, was simply to indicate that as a student, Althusser learned the most from the teacher whose rhetoric was attuned to the discourse of the arena in which he planned to make his career, and that the values and beliefs of his tutor proved far less consequential than the form in which he cast his thought and the personal integrity with which he held those beliefs. We have a different educational system in this country, and that system is in a different relation to political and economic structures of power. There would be no point in simply trying to replicate this foreign structure in our own environment. But those of our students who are aspiring to graduate and professional training are in situations analogous to that of the young Althusser. And we need to ask what will help such students when they make that next career move. We also need to ask where our other students are headed, and what we can give them that will prove not an encumbrance but a resource in the days ahead.

And where is "truth" in all this, you may well be thinking. Now he has run up his true colors, the Jolly Roger of sophistry and cynicism. On the contrary, my friends, I have been trying very hard to read Althusser rightly and to tell the truth about the meaning of his text as I understand it. The "love of truth" requires no less of me. Althusser found his truth in communism and in his own way of reading Marx, and, though it is not my truth, I honor him for finding it and presenting it so eloquently. But I honor him even more for trying, in this ultimate document of his life, to tell the truth about his own intellectual and emotional formation. The point of my little investigation into his development as a student and writer, however, is that truth is precisely what his teachers could not give him, though the best of them could give him a model of that love of truth and eloquence in its service that constitutes the integrity of our profession. Not to do violence to the realities we encounter by making them conform to some truth we think we know—that is the love of truth I am professing here.

We teachers of language and literature are mostly bourgeois subjects, engaged in trying to replicate ourselves in the service of government and corporate interests. Our job, as I see it, largely comes down to developing better bourgeois subjects—better than ourselves, that is, as well as better than they might be without our teaching. I am suggesting that we can diminish what I will call our hypocriticism by undertaking to do this job as honestly and decently as we can. One truth we know is that change will come, is coming. The values that we are used to assigning to individualism and collectivism, to freedom and conformity, are not forever fixed. We must prepare our students not just to accept change but to participate in bringing it about with the most enlightened sense of their interests—and larger interests—that we can help them to develop. We are not artisans shaping the impressionable minds of our students. We are—or should be— masters of our craft helping others to master it, and human beings of integrity helping others to achieve it in their own ways in their own lives.

For too long, we have designed curricula in order to do justice to what we perceived as our subject matter. What I am suggesting is that we stop thinking of ourselves as if we had a subject matter and start

CHAPTER THREE

What Is Becoming an English Teacher?

As you have seen, I begin with a question: "What is becoming an English teacher?" But this is not just one question. And it is not only a question. Without the question mark it might mean something like, "You are now about to learn what sorts of behavior are proper or attractive for those who teach English." Restore the question mark and the verbal formula is still open to a number of readings. For instance, it might be understood as raising a question about what sort of creatures are getting certified to teach English. Borrowing some language from William Butler Yeats, we might then pose the question in these terms: What rough beast, its hour come round at last, slouches toward graduate school to become an English teacher? In this form, our question is a less polite version of a more normal concern, namely, what sort of people are being attracted into this profession? Not a trivial question, even in its polite form, but somehow more striking when we acknowledge the possibility of "lower" forms of life entering the profession. Finally, though not exhaustively, my title raises the question of what it means to become, or rather—and this is important—to be becoming an English teacher.

I insist upon this awkward phrase—but let me pause here on this word *awkward*. (In this awkward pause, and throughout this chapter, I will be drawing on my own experience and adopting a frankly personal tone, because I am so deeply implicated in this topic that I can neither attain nor even pretend to objectivity. I will also be addressing my fellow teachers directly, for we are all in the same boat. I can only hope that this narrow focus will not prevent this chapter from being of some interest to those concerned about English but not directly involved in the teaching of it.) When I first started teaching English more than thirty years ago, we all learned a system of marking student papers that involved putting little signs or symbols into the margins to indicate the sins that had been committed inside the text. One of these signs of sin was the abbreviation *Awk,* for awkward, which we fledging teachers used, though our handbook did not admit this, whenever we felt there was something wrong with a bit of writing but could not say exactly what. In my first semester on the other side of the desk I flung *Awk*s at my students with wild abandon—until I discovered that many of them had not bothered to learn our little pedantic code but took my *Awk*s to be expressions of my own pedagogical emotion: a reaction of disgust to what they had written, something on the order of *Yuck*—or worse. This discovery shook me a bit, but at that time I could scarcely comprehend how right those students were, how well they understood the inner meaning of my *Awk*s. In fact, it took me years to begin to be troubled by the depth of my own ignorance about the subject I was supposed to be teaching. What I mean, then, by *becoming* an English teacher, includes a sense of one's own limitations, an awareness of how deep the sea of English is and how shallow and frail one's boat.

We English teachers, it seems, have apprenticed ourselves to a discipline we can never hope to master—which means that we must learn to enjoy reducing our clumsiness and ignorance without ever hoping to be perfectly graceful and wise. We must learn to enjoy the state of becoming, for we will never fully and perfectly *be* English teachers. Nevertheless, we need some idea of what it might mean to master this discipline. At the moment, in this great, gross, complicated, and confused country of ours, we are encumbered with too many ideas and ideals of education, some of which are absolutely at odds with one another, and also at odds with anything in the way of realistic expectations. I want to begin, then, by trying to get back to basics, if you will—but in the sense of trying to describe some fundamental core of belief and value that all of us who are English teachers can actually be said to share, in this country and at this time.

It may seem futile, if not obscene, to talk about ideals and goals while ignoring the practical problems that face most teachers of English in our public schools—problems that have to do with actual classroom conditions and with the lives students live outside of school, which powerfully influence the quality of attention those students can bring to any schooling we may offer them. Certainly, it is obscene to look at the world of public education in this country and seek to solve its problems by imposing some rigid national curriculum or by merely lengthening the school hour, the day, or the year. Let me assure you that I have no such unrealistic proposals to offer. On the other hand, if we are to explain our situation to the public and make the case for whatever reforms we ourselves think are necessary, we can do so only in terms of ideals and goals to which we can appeal. On this occasion, I want to share some thoughts with you about what it means to teach "English." I don't intend to lay down the law or insist that I know what is best for every teacher in the land, but to look for those common values that English teachers share with one another. Take what I say, I beg you, not as the Truth but as part of a dialogue that must go on among us all in the name of truthfulness—a dialogue conducted in the spirit of that love of truth without which our lives are empty and meaningless.

In speaking of ideals I propose to begin by asking my fellow teachers, for whom English has become a central part of their lives, what they remember about how this happened. In the choice between this academic subject and that one, between this field of study and that one, something important of what we are emerges, and in our professional commitment to such a field we may find what John Ruskin called in just such a connection "the Roots of Honour." In this spirit, asking English teachers to think back to their own attraction to English, I raise the question of what this profession, and those of us who profess it, actually stand for. We do stand for something, do we not, we who love English, who have come to consciousness and culture through this language, who have found in it not merely a medium of expression but a vocation, a calling, the professional center and public justification of our lives? We stand, I believe, for something far deeper than our particular curricular or institutional settings. We stand for whatever dignity this language can afford the human beings who find expression in and through it. We stand, above all, for sharing the powers and pleasures of this language with one another and with all those who seek our guidance in attaining those powers and pleasures. That is what I believe we stand for and I am certain that, though they might have much to add to what I have said, many English teachers share in that belief.

My readers may have noticed something missing in my brief exposition of where English teachers should take their stand. I would especially expect my fellow teachers to notice this, because even without the reminders of recent literary theory, English teachers have long been aware that the absences in texts are often as significant as the presences. In any case, I want to linger over this absence, to write it more firmly into my text. What I left out of my brief formulation of our commonly held ideal was the word *literature*. Furthermore, in talking about what is becoming an English teacher I have conspicuously failed to invoke the ideals of culture, taste, or spiritual uplift that have been a part of our rhetoric of self-promotion since the days of Hugh Blair. (See Court, 30–38, for a discussion of Blair's Edinburgh lectures of 1759–60, which were published in 1783 as *Lectures on Rhetoric and Belles Lettres*—a book which was still part of the Yale curriculum in 1823.) These omissions were deliberate, I assure you, and I shall return to the reasons for them before ending my discourse. But first I must ask you to consider some other matters, beginning with a further critical probe into the ideal vision I have just briefly sketched. A hostile critic—and we need to teach our students how to serve as their own hostile critics—might observe that my ideal, in addition to leaving out an essential element, is also generally vague and not likely to be of much use except in the loosely inspirational manner of certain sermons and political speeches. (As you can see,

tion of what is becoming an English teacher, then, has to do less with the sort of garments we might wear than with the sort of garments we may weave. And here we are approaching a paradox that lies at the heart of English teaching. What becomes us is an acceptance of our condition as unfinished beings, whose mode of presentation— garments in the metaphor we are weaving for the moment—must be subject to perpetual alteration. Thus nothing will ever fully and finally become us. This is why, in a certain sense, we cannot formulate a proper ideal for being an English teacher. We can, however, weave a wreath of words around this subject and cast it into the stream of time. Then we can begin weaving the next one. But one at a time. Weaving is a textual process, the creation of a textile or web out of mere threads. Let me weave, then, an image of the weaver weaving—an image of the English teacher as an instructor of textuality, a weaver of texts who teaches such weaving to others. And I propose this knowing that such a web, like Penelope's, will have to be undone and redone, because the weaver's work is never done.

The first strand in my web will be historical. (And here I shall simply look a bit more closely at certain aspects of the story that I told in Chapter 1.) As we have seen, when English began to be taught in the schools and colleges of these colonies three centuries ago, there was no such subject as English literature as we now understand it. Reading and writing the language was a school subject, and the grammar and oratorical uses of the language got some attention in college. But the colleges of New England, for instance, had no English requirements for entrance at all, and introduced English grammar as an entrance requirement only about a century and a half ago. A knowledge of English literature—as opposed to grammar—did not become an admission requirement at Brown University, for instance, until 1876. The whole English requirement at that time consisted of "the Analysis and Prosody of the First Act of Julius Caesar" (Bronson, 369). The first act of a single, highly rhetorical play! By 1881, however, entering students were required to know four whole works of

English literature: *Othello, The Vicar of Wakefield, The Deserted Village,* and *The Bride of Lammermoor.* They were required, that is to say, to know a single play by Shakespeare, prose and verse narratives by Oliver Goldsmith, and a novel by Sir Walter Scott.

If these requirements seem ludicrous now, it is because we have all been formed in a different set of beliefs—a set of beliefs that is, perhaps, beginning to seem ludicrous itself. I shall return to this question of ludicrousness, but for the moment let us pursue the history of English teaching a bit further. We can proceed by remembering that most colleges in this country did not even have departments of English until near the end of the nineteenth century. English literature was simply not seen as a necessary or serious subject. Classical orations, epic poems, and the great religious and philosophical texts took care of human values and morality, as well as what used to be called taste. Mathematics and the sciences developed the student's reasoning powers and opened the way to careers in business and technology. Oratory and rhetoric stressed the uses of language that might be needed by a preacher, legislator, or lawyer. What need was there for the study of English literature? No need at all. English literature entered the curriculum and flourished there only by taking the place of Latin and Greek texts, and by replacing the study of rhetoric with the study of criticism. A move, we should note, that decisively shifted the balance of emphasis from the production of texts to their reception. English literature also took over from Greek and Latin— and from the biblical texts as well—the major responsibility for developing in students that mysterious thing called taste, and part of the responsibility for inculcating the ethical values needed to sustain a meritocratic, entrepreneurial social and political structure.

I mention our social structure because it is the key to what has become of English as well as to what is becoming of it. What we used to call the American dream involved a vision of upward social and economic mobility—for everybody, regardless of logic and economic realities. That is, the dream required, with the logic of dreams but not of reason, that everyone should move upward and no one downward. I do not mean to sneer at this vision, because I have lived it myself. My mother was one of five sisters born to a young Italian couple who came to Brooklyn and died there in their youth. With the help of their priest and their community these five girls raised themselves, and four of them moved into the professional class by getting certified as school teachers. My father, of an Anglo-Irish family in Philadelphia, worked his way out of the Pennsylvania steel mills and into the life of a middle-class businessman. These parents sent me to better schools than they had attended themselves and made me the embodiment of their dream. Ultimately, they sent me to Yale University, that bastion of Capitalism and Protestantism (where, as I indicated in Chapter 1, I made up part of the 10 percent quota of Roman Catholics admitted in 1946). In that school, however, I did not become a Protestant, nor did I stubbornly persist in my native Catholicism. I learned instead, like many others, to find in literature a substitute for my church. Thus, in the last years of the 1940s, I was thoroughly indoctrinated into the religion of literature. That is, I came to believe, with others of my generation, that reading literature and criticizing it were the best things a human being could do with life (with the possible exception of producing literature that might lend itself profitably to such exacting critical scrutiny).

I present myself as an example here by way of acknowledging that I am implicated in the system of assumptions that I am about to criticize as no longer viable for English teachers. It is, at any rate, a faith in which I no longer can believe. I grew up in this system, I benefited from it, but I am deeply troubled by its inadequacies for our present situation. And when I speak of inadequacies, I am not just talking about some methodological problems that we can rectify by tinkering with our curriculum. I am talking about a set of assumptions about teaching that are so out of touch with our real situation as to be both ludicrous and dangerous. As Richard Ohmann began to tell us two decades ago (in *English in America*), the education that such young people as he and I received in college — and which was transmitted to the secondary schools via entrance requirements and such devices as the SATs and the Advanced Placement Tests in English — was an education that presupposed a life of moneyed leisure on the one hand and an acceptance of the social status quo on the other: not a life for the idle rich alone, to be sure, but a life that assumed the financial ease, the free time, and the excess energy required for serious aesthetic pursuits. Literature, under this regime of instruction, consisted of a set of verbal icons, the reverent study of which (something very close to worship) could save, or at least sustain, the souls of individuals otherwise buffeted or soiled by the hubbub of daily life. These assumptions scarcely allowed for the lawyer or manager who brings so much work home that serious reading or study is out of the question, not to mention anyone whose work is more physically demanding and whose need for entertainment more insistent.

What I am trying to suggest here (and in doing so I may only be reviving or developing the insights of Ohmann's important and perceptive book) is that the centrality of literature in our English curriculum was dependent upon two cultural assumptions that were not in themselves literary. One was the Arnoldian assumption that literature had become the scripture of modern civilization. And the other was the even less defensible assumption that the graduates of our literary curriculum would live sufficiently gracious lives for literature to remain intellectually and spiritually important in those lives. (A third assumption, that literary study was itself an excellent preparation for the world of business and affairs, I have already dealt with in Chapter 1.) Though I have somewhat more sympathy for the first of these two assumptions than for the second, I shall insist that they are both sadly mistaken. I shall argue, in fact, that if we English teachers are to become what we should, and do what becomes us, we must examine these assumptions critically and rid ourselves of them to the extent that we are able to do so. Let us examine them more closely.

In my parents' house there was some elegant furniture: the sort of objects that proved we had indeed attained the level of culture appropriate to the monied middle class. And on one elegant table in particular, I remember, there were always two decorative bookends, with four or five books bound in soft leather resting permanently between them. In the days when, like a giant locust, I was reading my way through everything in the house (imagine me as a sort Gregor Samsa with a voracious appetite for books), I finally reached the point where there was nothing left but these precious objects. I knew obscurely that they were meant to be seen and not read, but it was clear that they were books, and I was hungry. So I pounced upon them. What were they? I remember only two titles: *Ivanhoe* and *Pickwick Papers*—by no means the least readable books in the world. But these were on the thinnest of India paper and printed in the most elegant fine print. Furthermore, the culture out of which these texts had emerged was so foreign to me that I could not position myself as their receptive reader. I made some headway with *Ivanhoe,* I believe, but Dickens's facetious description of the Pickwick Club was as alien to me as the Egyptian *Book of the Dead.* Hungry as I was, I could scarcely sink my teeth into these texts. Like the piano in the bourgeois household of Jean Renoir's film about the tramp Boudu, these books were meant to be possessed and displayed, not to be used.

In college, of course, I learned that Scott and Dickens were not especially serious authors—not nearly so serious, for instance, as Henry James or T. S. Eliot—but the image of those sacred books pathetically representing a culture that my parents did not really possess still haunts me. And I am grateful to that cultural ghost for rising now to help me make concrete the problem of the assumptions that lay behind the teaching of literature in my school days. For I believe that the gift of literature, which my teachers tried to give me, was much like those books in my parents' house, and like the furniture in that house as well. That is, this gift of literature assumed a level of gracious living that had little or nothing to do with the actual condition of my life as it was going to be—so that this gift was all too likely

the person doing the dropping. I want to suggest that precisely this process is now occurring to the classics of English literature. They are being broken up, commodified, and packaged for handy consumption and recirculation. The infamous list of cultural nuggets proposed some years ago by E. D. Hirsch is nothing more than just such an attempt at packaging. Such texts as Cliff Notes are another. As our Romantic faith in the spiritual value of literary texts has waned, we have found ourselves more and more requiring knowledge *about* texts instead of encouraging the direct experience *of* these texts.

Another aspect of our situation has to do with the English curriculum itself and the internal dynamic of the professional study of English literature. The English curriculum that came into being around the turn of the nineteenth century is still the English curriculum. There have been adjustments in emphasis, to be sure, and many additions. Modern English and American literature have grown in relation to earlier English literature. Gender and ethnic considerations have resulted in additions to the canon. Colonial and postcolonial literatures in English have been acknowledged. And the discipline has to some extent theorized itself and built such theorizing into the curriculum. But courses in Chaucer, Shakespeare, Milton, the Romantics, and so on are still the backbone of the English curriculum. Though much has been added, not so much has been taken away. Moreover, a century of professionalism in literary studies has resulted in a huge body of secondary writing in the form of bibliographies, biographies, and interpretations. Even someone dedicated to the study of a single major writer like Joyce or Woolf can scarcely keep up with all the secondary literature in so narrow a field, let alone read everything their author wrote and much of what he or she read, and otherwise master the milieu in which this writer was formed. There is now so much written material associated with English and American literature that an enormous gap has become apparent between the ideal knowledge of the field and the actual knowledge attained by English majors, by graduate students, and even by faculty. Under the weight of all this "scholarship" it has become more and more difficult to pretend that literary study is a progressive discipline. We are forgetting as fast as we learn, and the processes of scholarship are now more clearly visible not as stages toward a more perfect knowledge but as fashions motivated by the need for change itself. One result of all this has been to turn us into professional hypocritics.

Hypocriticism is a word whose time has come. It acknowledges more fully than is usual the roots of *hypocrite* in the ancient Greek verb *hypokrino,* which had a set of meanings sliding from simple speech, to orating, to acting on stage, to feigning or speaking falsely. We are constantly in danger of following the same trajectory. I propose this word, then, to refer to a weak and deficient kind of criticism —and also, of course, as in the normal usage of the word *hypocrisy,* to refer to what *Webster's Collegiate* calls the "act or practice of feigning to be what one is not or to feel what one does not feel; esp. the false assumption of an appearance of virtue or religion." Hypocriticism is simply the critical practice of people who must go through motions developed by evangelical teachers like Billy Phelps without the faith that animated Phelps himself, who know less literature than Phelps did because they must know more critical theory and can't, after all, know everything, and who have lost faith in the possibility of either themselves or the books they "profess" telling the truth about anything important in the lives of those they are teaching. We hypocritics have lost faith in what we do, which means we must either recover that faith or change what we are doing. As should be obvious by now, I believe that the only way to recover faith in ourselves and our project is indeed to change what we are doing, for our present enterprise is a leaky vessel, and the vessel is adrift in a culture almost as indifferent to its fate as the ocean itself.

A boat adrift, however, is still a boat, and no one is going to climb out of it to follow some swimmer who claims that land is just over the horizon. The prudent castaway will hang on to that boat. For English teachers the boat is our belief in what we may usefully think of as the Story of English—a narrative that begins with *Beowulf* and now concludes perhaps with Geoffrey and Tobias Wolff. The Story of English is divided into chapters we call periods. Each period must be "covered" for the story of English to be complete. And, because we are professionals, each period must be covered by an "expert," a person who, in addition to knowing the whole story, is especially knowledgeable about his or her own chapter or period. This means that every college English department can be measured by its ability to personify the whole story with expertise if not eminence in each period. English departments live by this Story. It is the Story we tell to deans when we want to hire a new faculty member or replace an old one. We are a chain that cannot afford a single weak link, whether it be in the later Middle Ages or in the early Romantic poets. As the primary and secondary canons swell, the links get smaller and smaller. A serious department with a graduate program must have someone "in" Shakespeare, of course, but also someone (usually someone else) "in" non-Shakespearean Elizabethan and Jacobean drama, and another someone in nondramatic literature of the English Renaissance, which field can now be divided into Henrician, Elizabethan, Jacobean, and Caroline specialties.

With every additional subdivision—each of which makes sense within the logic of professionalization—we are driven deeper and deeper into hypocriticism, for every move toward greater specialization leads us away from the needs of the majority of our students and drives a larger wedge between our professional lives and our own private needs and concerns. Even the New Historicism, which is one of the bravest flowers in the garden (or is it a jungle?) of poststructuralism, seems rooted in a historical period in which the lines of power organize themselves around a visible monarch—which makes all its learning and cleverness of questionable usefulness for our attempts to understand the confused dynamics of power in our own world. If the New Historicism is a very sophisticated way of clinging to the Story of English, just as the New Criticism was a very sophisticated way of clinging to a Romantic notion of the poem as Spirit's dwelling place, we can see in their shared adjective of temporality a way of concealing the fact that neither of them could be as New as they both wished to be.

The sophisticated moves of the newest modes of critical theory are proving unable to save us from hypocriticism. They have, in fact, contributed mightily to it in their own ways, which, though they are different from and even opposed to the older modes of thought, often put us as teachers in a position equally false. I must speak crudely and hastily here, but the charge I am about to make could be developed at greater length (as it was, to some extent, in Chapter 2). Many modes of poststructuralist thought privilege the unconscious, the irrational, the anarchical, the primitive, the illogical, the ungrammatical, the antisocial, the strange, the mad, the destructive, the outlawed. Without denying in myself some sympathy for aspects of these views, I want to observe that most of the people expressing them have made their own accommodations with society, with order, with institutions upon which they depend in order to function as they do. To the extent that these radical critiques, made from safe and tenured positions, may lead students to take chances that can damage their lives, those of us who make them are practicing hypocriticism of the poststructuralist sort, which is no prettier than any other form of hypocritical behavior.

One answer to Jacques Derrida's questions — "Are we responsible? For what and to whom?" — is that we are responsible to our students. And for what? For helping them to find what they need to get from their academic studies. What our students need, as I see it, is first of all some guidance in learning how to understand their world and survive in it, and secondarily some grounds for criticizing and trying to improve it. Excessive radicalism may be better than excessive traditionalism — but it is not much better. We have proved unwilling to give up our claims to special status as interpreters of quasi-sacred texts and unable to replace our pragmatic need to justify departmental structures founded on the historical narrative of the Story of English. And we are also unwilling to relinquish those comparable assertions, based upon the magical powers of literary theory, which now function in many cases simply as a new way of claiming the old status. It is the disparities between our professional needs and our personal desires, as well as the gap between our pedagogical practices and the needs of our students, that turn us into hypocritics. The remedy, I want to suggest, is to rethink our practice by starting with the needs of our students rather than with our inherited professionalism or our personal preferences. To understand the needs of our students we shall have to face more squarely than we usually do our present cultural situation.

And what is our present cultural situation? Without pretending to full command of such complexity (which would be hypocriticism with a vengeance), I expect you to agree with me that we— teachers as well as students—live in a society that is more fully and insistently textualized than anything people have experienced in the past. Human beings have, since prehistoric times, existed as cultural animals, of course, in social contexts that were mediated by symbolic structures. But it is impossible to deny that language and other semiotic systems and their associated media of communication have in the course of history multiplied and penetrated more and more deeply into our daily lives. We are at present, like it or not, the most mediated human beings ever to exist on this earth. It is abundantly clear, moreover, that to function as a citizen of these United States one needs to be able to read, interpret, and criticize texts in a wide range of modes, genres, and media. What our students need to function in such a world, then, is an education for a society still struggling to balance its promises of freedom and equality, still hoping to achieve greater measures of social justice, still trying not to homogenize its people but to allow for social mobility and to make the lower levels of its economic structure tolerable and humane. This is a political program of sorts—but it is not a program for another revolution. Its goal is to contribute toward making good on the still unfulfilled promises of the first American revolution—or, at the very least, to resist the erosion of what has already been achieved.

This program is not strictly the responsibility of teachers of language and literature, but the highly textualized and mediated nature of our society has constructed for such teachers a position of great importance as educators—if we are willing to change our discipline so as to occupy this position. This means, I should say, letting go of the Story of English as our main preoccupation, and giving up our role as exegetes of quasi-religious texts. It also means giving up any claim to be revolutionary opponents of "the system." We are in it and of it, and we had better admit this to ourselves and others, just to clear the air. The glamour that has attended the notion of "literature" itself for the past two centuries is just one of the things we must renounce. The glamour of "theory" is another. Which doesn't mean that we must forget what we have learned—but we must put our learning to use, for instance, by beginning to deconstruct the opposition between the "English" courses and the "service" courses taught by English departments.

Service courses, like the service entrances of mansions, are for those benighted folk who are not permitted to use the front door. In our case that means we distinguish sharply, and on a basis very close to social class, between those who seek to become like us (our English majors) and those with whom we must deal as lesser breeds whom we agree, for a price, to "sivilize"—which makes us the Aunt Pollies of American education. At present we deal with this situation in English departments mainly by consigning such courses to a lower class of teachers—adjuncts and graduate students—replicating within our departments the class structure that we impose upon our students. This is bad enough, but what we do in our "nonservice" courses is even worse. There we assume that what is good for those intent on becoming English teachers is also good for everybody else. The traditional English major is designed for young people entering

assignment 3

"So Happy a Skill"

This is the third version of a lecture about the teaching of writing delivered to two different audiences. My first audience was a conference of writing teachers. My second was a group of college students and their faculty. The function of the piece in this, its new and final location, is to demonstrate how some of the notions of text and textuality presented in other parts of this book might play out in an ordinary college writing classroom.

My topic today is academic writing: that is, the kind of writing done by college students in their classes and by college faculty in their fields of study. In discussing this topic I shall make several assumptions that I want to share with you at the beginning of my talk. First, I assume that academic writing is not only something that students must learn how to do in their own self-defense during their college years but that it also ought to be a useful mental discipline that college graduates can draw upon, directly or indirectly, for the rest of their lives. Second, I assume that the students and faculty in any academic discipline ought to be doing the same kind of writing, so that the faculty in sociology, for example, should feel responsible for helping students to write like sociologists, just as the faculty in English should be responsible for helping students to write as they themselves write. Finally, I assume that it is reasonable for me to talk to an audience of students and faculty about my own problems as a writer and about the way that writing should be taught and studied in college.

My procedure will be a bit unusual. I am going to present you with a bit of writing that I wrote originally for another occasion. This, I should hasten to say, is not in itself a bit unusual. Academic lecturers are forever recycling the same talks, changing them slightly to suit different audiences, firmly convinced that God created word processors to encourage this very practice. Personally, I know that the devil invented word processors, but that is beside the point. What will be unusual in my recycling of a talk originally written for another occasion is that I will not try to hide the fact but will offer you exactly the talk I originally delivered, except for the correction of a few errors I found while reading it aloud. When I wrote this talk for that other occasion, I also knew that I would deliver it here, and knew that it would have to be reframed, so to speak, to function properly for this occasion. And that is what I am doing right now—reframing my talk. (And, of course, I have re-re-framed it for this book.)

I hope you will bear with me in what may seem an excessive self-consciousness here. I ask this indulgence because I am trying to use my own writing as a way of discussing the problems of all academic writing: to deliver a lecture on academic writing and to discuss the writing of that very lecture as an example of the problems every academic writer must face and of the kinds of solution one may hope to find. My first problem was finding a title. All of us who give lectures must often provide titles long before we get down to the writing of the lecture itself. This can pose problems, but academic writers become adept at generating evasive titles—and also at explaining to audiences why the lecture they are about to give is indeed on a topic quite different from that implied by the title. In my case—and here I am sharing with you information I deliberately withheld from the first audience for this lecture—at the moment when I was asked to address a particular topic for a conference of teachers of writing, I happened to be studying a quite different topic. Let me tell you about this.

I was working on the writing of British women in the first part of the twentieth century, taking a special interest in their attempts to gain some control over definitions of gender and patterns of sexual behavior. My study of *The Well of Loneliness,* a lesbian novel that was successfully prosecuted for obscenity by the British government, led me to the work of the early sexologist Havelock Ellis, one of whose books had also been the victim of successful prosecution by the government, and whose theories are usually thought to have had a bad effect on the novel in question. In looking into Ellis's life and works—which are equally strange and wonderful, I might add—I came across an essay called "The Art of Writing," which I was reading at the very moment when I had to supply a title for my talk on writing. Hitting upon the happy phrase "so happy a skill" in that essay, in a paragraph from which some interesting ideas could be extracted, I chose that phrase as my title, intending, at some point in my lecture, to produce it (along with Ellis himself) as a rhetorical rabbit from my textual hat.

The phrase, as you shall learn in due course, concerns a matter of what semioticians call intertextuality, and, because I meant to give intertextuality a central place in my lecture, I considered my discovery of it to be a serendipitous one. In the actual writing, as it happened, one thing led to another and it was some time before I got around to my title phrase, but it helped me to begin. It gave me a feeling that a destination had been prepared which I need only persevere to reach. Academic writers, whether veterans or rookies, need such things, which is why I mention it. This phrase, and the passage in which it was embedded, was all the outline I had when I began writing, but it served its purpose, helping me both to get started and to get finished. And now, I must start in earnest or we shall never get finished today. For the rest of this time you will be overhearing a lecture initially aimed at an audience of writing teachers.

My title, "So Happy a Skill," is a borrowed expression, a quotation. And that is appropriate, for I mean to take up the topic of how texts are made out of other texts. Part of my aim in this discussion will be to argue that this whole matter of intertextuality should be central in any attempt to do what is usually called "teaching writing." For reasons that I shall try to make apparent in the course of this essay, I do not believe that we can actually teach writing, though I do indeed believe that we can help people to improve as writers if they desire such improvement. Though I think this holds true for all writing, I am only claiming here that any course designed to help students negotiate the challenges of *academic* writing (which is, after all, the subject of our conference) should give a central place to the theory and practice of intertextuality. I am also very much aware— in this time and place how could I not be?—that as I write this, I am also producing a piece of academic writing myself, one that will have to be read aloud on at least one occasion and then possibly appear in print later on. In this discussion, though I hope to avoid becoming paralyzed with self-consciousness, I intend to connect my problems in producing an academic paper like this one to the problems faced by every student who writes an academic paper.

Like any student's paper, this one was produced in response to an assignment and for a deadline or series of deadlines. After agreeing, in a general way, to do something at this conference, which is very like enrolling in a particular course, I received a letter from Pat Sullivan giving me a more specific assignment: a paper that could be delivered in thirty minutes and would draw upon my "interest in issues of text and context and in processes of reading and writing." I was also given a deadline for submission of a title and an admonition not to "report on work that has been promised for publication elsewhere." Borrowing some terminology from Michael Baxandall's book on the interpretation of artworks, *Patterns of Intention,* I was given not just a *charge*— "write a paper, deliver a talk"—but a *brief* that put the charge in terms of what Baxandall calls "local conditions in the specific case" (30).

At the risk of disrupting both your and my continuity of thought here, I must stop and ask, "Why Baxandall?" What has an art historian's discussion of the building of a bridge over the Firth of Forth in Scotland got to do with the problems of writing? That is—why did I, as a writer working on an assignment, feel a need to call upon

Baxandall's aid? Well, "Got to fill up these thirty minutes," to be sure, just as our students feel they must fill up whatever quota of words or pages they are asked to produce. But there is more to it than that. I want to suggest that much of what students have to learn about academic writing comes down to the process that brings something like my citation of Baxandall into this text. As I was trying to find the words to explain the intertextual situation of every writer, Baxandall's explanation of compositional process simply drifted into my mind, as a simple, clear, and powerful way of describing how texts actually get produced. What I liked about his book when I first read it was that it took a problem in civil engineering as a model for discussing the production of paintings, moving from the building of the Forth bridge to paintings by Picasso, Chardin, and Piero della Francesca.

Part of what interested me in Baxandall's book was the fact that he used the model of a utilitarian work with some aesthetic dimension—the building of a bridge—as a way of getting a clearer look at the production of more fully aesthetic visual texts. It was this way of connecting the practical and the aesthetic, I now understand, that made Baxandall's book memorable for me, because it was connected by analogy to problems of reading and writing that I regularly face as a writer and a teacher. For my citation of Baxandall to be justified in the present circumstance, however, I shall have to work with it, do something with it to make it productive in terms of my particular brief on this occasion. I will go further and say that if I couldn't find anything to do with it other than to cite or mention it, that it would be an error to bring it into my text. We academic writers must learn both that we have no choice but to be intertextual and also that we are obliged to add our own labor to these intertexts in order to make them do productive work in helping us with our own textual problems. We need them. We cannot do without them. But we must use them, work them, in order to get beyond mere quotation. In the case of my use of some words of Baxandall's, my effort takes the form of adapting his terminology to my rather different context. Often, in

purpose of developing this fluency. That is, assignments must not be grossly beyond the capacities of those asked to perform them, and yet they should extend and develop those capacities. A major purpose of writing courses is precisely to expand the element of "culture" for students taking such courses. This is a mere platitude, however, unless we can be more specific about how to undertake such expansion. Once again, Baxandall can help us.

His notion of culture specifically includes "models (both positive and negative)." You don't build a bridge without knowing something about how bridges have been built, including those that have fallen into the rivers they were supposed to span. An important negative model for the Forth project was a bridge built in the 1870s across the Firth of Tay, which "blew over in an easterly gale, taking a passenger train with it" (17). This negative example proved to be extremely helpful in planning a bridge designed for similar conditions: but one that would not fall down. The successful designer of the Forth bridge also knew of many good examples of bridge building, though none of them exactly matched his brief. Translated to our own situation, the proper use of models means that students of writing should see and discuss some examples of good and bad writing of the sort required by their own assignments. We are, of course, very familiar with the use of good examples. In our literature courses we habitually teach only good examples, since our notion of *literature* does not allow us to modify that noun with the adjective *bad*. There is no bad literature. The result of this is that English teachers are accustomed to finding only good things in the works that they assign and lots of bad things in the assignments students compose for them. What do you do with a student's assignment? You "correct" it, do you not? But how often do you "correct" a poem, play, story, or even an essay that is part of your syllabus? Not very often, I should think.

This is a real problem. Verbal texts seldom fall into the Tay, carrying a train of readers with them. We are more familiar with essays resembling trains that huff and puff a lot but never seem to get out of the station. (At this moment, for instance, I am worrying about whether my own engine has enough power to make it up the gentle slope we are presently climbing.) If we accept Baxandall's view that bad examples are important, how can we ensure that our students encounter some of these and understand the causes of their badness? To begin with, I want to reject as counterproductive the two most obvious ways of finding bad examples to use in a writing course. I do not think that we can do a good job of finding published essays that are bad in useful ways. Even Brooks and Warren had a terrible time finding bad poems to discuss in *Understanding Poetry,* and they fell all over themselves trying to show why such poems were indeed bad. If we select material that we simply don't like, we run the risk of selecting what other people, including our students, may like very well—which can lead to mere debating of prejudices rather than useful criticism. On the other hand, if we select writing by students to serve as our bad examples, we may simply reinforce the frustration and hostility of those students. Such writing may also fail to be bad in instructive, creative ways.

No—to find really helpful sorts of badness, we shall have to produce bad texts ourselves. First, though, we must face the fact that badness is never absolute. It is always a matter of context, purpose, function. If one wished to design a bridge so as to create a disaster, the Tay bridge would have been an excellent solution. Similarly, the most feeble and ungrammatical sentence might, in the proper context, be a perfect example of a feeble and ungrammatical sentence. (Let me point out, parenthetically, here, that once I have introduced the good and bad bridges into my text I can keep drawing upon them for illustrations that lend specificity and point to my discourse. The bridge and the train have been working for me in more ways than one: as analogies, metaphors, and concrete illustrations of the points I am trying to make—including this one. I did not know, when I brought the train into my text how it would be used, but once it had arrived I could use it to get from there to here. Such use is what I mean by making borrowed textual matter earn its keep to justify the borrowing.)

Returning from my meta-discourse, I must try to get back on the right track. I am arguing that academic writing, like bridge building, must be done in the light of previous examples—good and bad—of the kind of work that is being done. Students who are asked to write about anything at all must have a chance to see how that kind of writing is done, and to study both good and bad examples of it. All academic writing, whether done by students or faculty, involves entering a conversation already in progress. Old veterans like myself may have been involved in certain conversations long enough to pick them up again as one resumes talking to an old friend, but younger writers, who are relatively new to certain topics and the ways they have been shaped, must be given specific and formal access to the way objects are constituted by the discourses around them. Even a poem is a poem not merely because of what poets do when they write but also because of the way poets, critics, and other readers regularly talk and write about poems. A piece of academic prose, then, is never simply in a relation to its object—to whatever it is writing about. It is also, always and already, in a relation to the ways in which its object has been written about and is currently being written about.

Looking at examples is a first necessity. The second necessity is some discussion about what makes for good and bad writing within the discourse in question. On this matter I am suggesting that we know quite well how to find good examples of writing to discuss but must find better ways of providing bad examples for study. The solution I propose is that teachers should take at least one well-formed example of a solution and deform it creatively before presenting it to students. In doing this we may lop crucial paragraphs, introduce feeble sentences, weaken connections, alter evidence—do whatever we wish that will enable us to analyze the resulting text with critical authority—because it is our own. I would recommend performing such an analysis, then taking questions about it, and finally producing the original as a good solution to the problems noted in the analysis. Having made the errors ourselves, we are in a position to resist claims that they are really improvements, since we know the ways in which they have weakened the original text we have warped to our purposes.

As I have suggested, preparing our malformed text requires some creative ability. Do all teachers of writing have this ability? My answer to this crucial question is that they must—they simply must. If we cannot make bad texts out of good ones, how can we hope to aid our students in improving their own written work? In actuality, I think many teachers have creative talent that may currently be unused and frustrated when they teach what we have called composition, or may even be misused simply because it cannot be repressed. In the example before us, in which a weakened piece of writing is discussed before the original is presented, a creative teacher may then be tempted to go further and subject the original itself to a devastating critique. I would resist this temptation for one simple reason. We do not want to set perfection before our students as their goal. We should not want to do this because we cannot teach perfection. Our range, our capabilities, go no further than craft. Even in "creative" writing courses, craft is all that can be taught. Any snatching of graces beyond the reach of art—as a crafty poet once put it—our students must do on their own. Our aim should be to help students learn how to produce a good, workmanlike job with a written essay whenever they need to. And this means what it means in any trade or craft. It means knowing what to avoid. It means using rules of thumb and tricks of the trade to accomplish basic tasks without having to think them out from scratch every time. It means mastering a medium through the study of models. In this particular case, it also means that we should select a good essay to deform rather than one we consider faulty.

The use of negative models can actually be taken one step further. After one such model has been discussed, it may be extremely helpful to ask students themselves to produce a deformed version of one of the positive models that is under discussion. This means involving students in a creative process of the negative sort, which can be as much fun as knocking down a tower of blocks or a house of cards—and requires a higher degree of skill. To learn not by doing, but by undoing, is the idea here. Specifically, in this kind of assignment, we should give students a brief that requires them to take a text that performs its function well and to sabotage it creatively so that it fails in ways that can be discussed as plausible examples of how writing can go astray. This can be done with whole texts or parts; it can be limited to certain features, such as diction or transitions. Many variations can be played on this basic theme. The point is to learn how a certain kind of text works by deliberately sabotaging that kind of text—not just writing another text about the first one, which we usually call textual analysis, but by actually intervening in the first text to produce another that exhibits certain carefully defined problems or weaknesses. This is analysis with a vengeance— a more effective form of analysis because more creative.

Up to now, we have been considering one dimension of what Baxandall calls "culture": the medium itself, as it may be studied through the use of positive and negative models. We must now consider at least one other major aspect of culture in order to complete even a rough sketch of the model of instruction on which we are working. Culture, as we are using the word here, means knowledge about the topic to which the brief is addressed, including, in particular, previous treatments of it. It is to avoid the problems of culture that writing instructors so often resort to assignments in which students are asked to write about themselves and their personal experiences, or "what they know." This kind of writing can be very instructive, but only, in my view, if it leads to exploration of the boundaries of the self as produced by culture and those resistances to social construction that constitute a unique subjectivity or individuality. What we know about ourselves is largely what our culture has enabled us to know—just as those selves are mainly the selves that our culture has enabled us to have. What is "real"—what is permanent about ourselves—may be only our resistance, our negation, our fear, our depression, our boredom. Finding a way to textualize these resistances is never easy. It requires effort, and a knowledge about the culture in which we have come to selfhood. That is one reason why we go to school: to come into possession of our selves by learning about our culture. All of which means that the apparently simple assignment of writing about one's self is far from simple, is actually quite difficult for both student and teacher to deal with productively.

A second problem with the personal writing assignment is that the writer's self is simply not what most academic writing is about. As I said, it has its place, but it should not usurp the place of the less obviously interesting task of learning how to write academic prose. Most academic writing specifically extends beyond the writer's self because it directly involves the extension of knowledge. Writing in the academy is a major way of extending knowledge by subjecting mere information to the disciplines of a particular discourse, with its attendant grammar and rhetoric. This means that most of the time, in the academic lives of both students and faculty, when we write, this writing is not directly about ourselves, or even about something that we already know entirely, but is directed toward the boundaries of our knowledge where discoveries may be made. The more we know about a field of study, of course, the more our discoveries are likely to be of interest to others, but the process of discovery can be exciting in itself. It has a formal quality that can give even a beginner's discoveries a structure that is engaging for the reader. But even a beginner must start with some sense of how a given discourse is conducted and what its major presuppositions are supposed to be. How to tackle a relatively new field of study is one of the things we have to teach. This is why intertextuality must be at the center of our teaching.

Texts are made mainly out of other texts. This does not mean that there is never anything new under the sun but that even something very new indeed must be presented in a textual form that is largely borrowed from other texts. In the academy the introduction to intertextuality received by most students takes the form of a stern warning against plagiarism. In a culture organized around property, patents, and copyrights, plagiarism has become a sin, occasionally a crime. In other cultures, or in certain contexts within our own, this sin does not exist. Certainly Chaucer and Shakespeare never worried about it. Alphonse Legros, who directed the Slade School of Art in London at the turn of the nineteenth century used to advise his students, "Si vous volez, il faut voler aux riches, et pas aux pauvres" ("If you steal, you must steal from the rich and not from the poor" — Holroyd, 40). And T. S. Eliot is famous for having observed that "immature poets imitate; mature poets steal" (Eliot, 125). If even painters and poets must operate intertextually, how much more so must this be the case with writers engaged on more academic topics?

At this point I want to reproduce some remarks on our topic by a writer who had a great success almost a century ago, writing on an astonishing range of subjects, though he is not much remembered now. He was a schoolmaster under trying circumstances; he earned a degree in medicine, though he did not practice for long; he suffered the ignominy of having a book successfully prosecuted for obscenity by the British government. He wrote on literature and on scientific subjects. He wrote essays and poems. He even wrote on writing, and it is from an essay of his called "The Art of Writing" that I have taken the title for this little talk. Let me quote the relevant passage from this essay. In this passage the author has been considering the notion that great writers seldom quote others. He acknowledges that this may often be the case but then goes on to make a rather different point.

> The significant fact to note, however, is not that the great writer rarely quotes, but that he knows how to quote. Schopenhauer was here a master. He possessed a marvelous flair for fine sayings in remote books, and these he would now and again let fall like jewels on his page, with so happy a skill that they seem to be

created for the spot on which they fell. It is the little
writer rather than the great writer who seems never to
quote, and the reason is that he is really never doing
anything else. (Ellis, 145)

The happy skill invoked here is that of a specific case of intertextuality, the actual quotation of one author by another, done in such
a way as to make the old gems appear to have been designed for
their new setting. We must assume something like this notion to be
operating in Eliot's admonition to steal rather than imitate, which is
really advice to make the old textual material thoroughly a part of the
new text. But we, as writers and teachers of writing, do not have to
do with greatness, since we can neither aim at it ourselves nor claim
to lead our students to it. We have everything to do with littleness,
which is why the last part of the quoted passage may be more important for us than the happy phrase I have borrowed for my title. The
little writer, we are told, seems never to quote because "he is really
never doing anything else."

The author I have been quoting here considered himself an original genius, I am sure, and with some justice, even though he is now
scarcely more than a footnote in those disciplines to which he contributed. (And I am deliberately leaving him anonymous to emphasize that fact.) Still, we can learn something from his admonitions—
if we are willing to face up to the littleness of our task. We academics
are mainly little writers ourselves, who are attempting to guide our
students into the ways of successful littleness as well. Fluency within
discursive bounds is the goal of academic writing, and staying within
discursive bounds involves a lot of semiconscious quotation. We have
as our goal—and the goal of each student—the achievement of littleness. Our students must learn to write as the Others write, in order
to survive in academic life. That is one side of our dilemma. The
other side is that, without some feeling of moving beyond the already
written, it is scarcely possible for a writer to write. This problem is

particularly acute for students, who are often poignantly aware of
the limits of their own knowledge and are confronted by academic
discourses that seem to be boundless. The dilemma, then, takes the
form of the inevitability of littleness versus the need of every writer—
even a fledgling writer—to feel that littleness is not inevitable.

This is a dilemma that immersion in a discipline over a long
period of time is designed to solve. By long study we academics hope
to reach the margins of our disciplines where our methods and our
learning come face to face with the raw chaos the discipline is designed to master. Many of us never quite reach this boundary, though
we sometimes convince ourselves that we have done so. Some of us
come to believe that, like Henry James's beast in the jungle, raw
chaos does not lie in wait at the end of our journey but paces beside us every step of the way. And others come to think that there
has never been any raw chaos, except what we have invented as the
untamed Other of our disciplined thinking. But whether the beast is
real or invented, beside us or distant, the trick is obviously to find it
and capture it in our textual nets, alive, if possible.

(I have been driven to metaphor here as a way of inducing a discursive beast into my textual net, but that action itself—the making
of a metaphor aided by a dim recollection of Henry James—is, even
as I write this passage, leading me to reformulate the textual and
pedagogical problem itself, rejecting the sharp distinction between
great and little, between quotation and originality.) The happy skill
needed by every writer struggling in the net of textuality is not so
much the art of quotation as the ability to push language toward
its metaphorical limits. Perhaps there is no way to get beyond quotation, to stretch the bonds of littleness, that is not metaphorical.
What is outside textuality may not be there waiting for us to throw
our perfected net of language over it, but may be brought into being
only by the charm of the net itself, appearing only where we have
playfully weakened or stretched the fabric, shaping the material of
the net itself into the beast we need to find. (If I may draw back

parenthetically from my own writing once again, I find that the textual play of the words I have brought into my discourse is leading me toward an unforeseen conclusion. I got to this point in my text driven by a brief and drawing upon a culture or discursive field that includes my experience as a teacher and writer, but in attempting to solve the problem set by my brief, I was led through a process of revision and rethinking in which I learned to loosen up a bit and play with my metaphors until their object came more clearly into view. This part of my text has been the most revised and has become for me the most interesting part. Even here, however, I would not claim to have escaped littleness and quotation, but I have rearranged my textual furniture a bit.)

In the course of writing these words, like any student, I have kept one eye upon my brief, including the length of time allotted me. Thirty minutes translates into fifteen pages, which translates into 27,000 characters, helpfully counted for me by Mr. Macintosh. At the moment we stand at 28,120 (in the "inner" text, that is). I shall conclude, then, with just two bits of advice. We must find topics for our writing courses that enable students to focus on their culture at the points where it most clearly impinges upon them, where they already have tacit knowledge that needs only to be cultivated to become more explicit. And in our teaching we should focus on the way that the topic of any course exists as the object of a discourse, a body of texts connected by a certain way of naming its objects that is ultimately metaphorical. The academic writer must learn to understand, use, and ultimately play with those metaphors. The skill of a writer is a happy one because it is based upon play.

CHAPTER FOUR

A Flock of Cultures
A Trivial Proposal

> The pigs were ranged on one side, the dogs on an-
> other, and then from a third a flock of cultures crept
> up from time to time.
>
> — *From the French printer's first attempt to set William
> Carlos Williams's* The Great American Novel

I t is tempting to read the French printer's creative typography
as an allegory of contemporary education: pigs on the right,
dogs on the left, and a flock of cultures timidly trying to find
a place among them. Are all those creatures, perhaps, feeding
on the rotting carcass of Western Civilization? Other interpretations may well occur to you. Feel free—this is not a classic text;
it lacks authority and intentionality. My own reading of it, however, reminds me of what a contested field education is today, how
polarized and politicized it has become, how difficult it is to speak
reasonably and effectively about a coherent core of study for college
students. Nevertheless, this is just what I propose to undertake in
this chapter. Specifically, I hope to explain just why such concepts as
Great Books and Western Civ cannot really solve the problem of our
"flock of cultures," and then I shall go on to make a "trivial proposal"
for a different core of humanistic study for college students. The ar-
rogance of such a gesture is all too apparent. In my own defense I
can only say that it is accompanied by a comparable amount of humility. I do not expect to solve our problems here, only to advance
our discussion of them beyond the point of mutual accusations and
recriminations.

Our problem as I see it—that is, the problem of college instruction in general and any humanistic core for such studies in particu-

lar—can be put in the form of two questions. It is my hope that those concerned about education, whether they are on the "right" or the "left," might agree that it is reasonable to see our problems in this manner. One question is how we can put students in touch with a usable cultural past. The other is how we can help students attain an active relationship with their cultural present. These two questions are intimately related, of course. We cannot answer one without taking a position on the other. Therefore, I shall try to consider them both, though my proposal is concerned mainly with the second. To approach the matter of a usable cultural past, I shall have to begin with questions of canonicity. This may at first seem like just another assault on Western Civ and the Great Books, but I ask for your patience. This is a different kind of critique, I believe, and it will have a different outcome than is usual. To begin with, however, we will need to have a clear understanding of the cultural role of canons. Let us begin at the beginning.

In ancient Greek we find the two words from which the modern English word *canon* (in its two spellings, *canon* and *cannon*) has descended: *kanna:* reed; and *kanōn:* straight rod, bar, ruler, reed (of a wind organ), rule, standard, model, severe critic, metrical scheme, astrological table, limit, boundary, assessment for taxation (Liddell and Scott). Like *canon,* our word *cane* is also clearly a descendant of the ancient *kanna,* but its history has been simpler and more straightforward than that of its cognate. The second of the two Greek words, on the other hand, has from ancient times been the repository of a complex set of meanings, mainly acquired by metaphorical extensions of the properties of canes, which are a set of hollow or tubular grasses, some of which are regularly jointed (like bamboo), and some of which have flat outside coverings. The tubular channel characteristic of reeds or canes leads to the associations of the word *canon* with functions that involve forcing liquids or gases through a channel or pipe, while their regularity and relative rigidity lead toward those meanings that involve measuring and controlling (ruling—in both senses of that word). And it is likely that the ready applicability of canes as a weapon of punishment (as in our verb *to cane,* or beat with a stick) supported those dimensions of the meaning of *kanōn* that connote severity and the imposition of power.

In Latin we find the same sort of meanings for the word *canon* as were attached to the Greek *kanōn,* with two significant additions, both coming in later Latin. These two additions are due to historical developments that generated a need for new terms. On the one hand, the rise of the Roman Catholic Church as an institution required a Latin term that could distinguish the accepted or sacred writings from all others, so that "works admitted by the rule or canon" came themselves to be called canonical or, in short, the Canon. In this connection we also find a new verb, *canonizare,* to canonize. On the other hand, with the importation of gunpowder and the development of artillery, the tubular signification of the word led to its becoming the name (in late Latin) for large guns (Lewis and Short). A common theme in these extensions is power.

For our purposes, what is significant in this is the way that *canon* in Latin also combined the meanings of rule or law with the designation of a body of received texts. In its Christian signification, however, *canon* came to mean not only a body of received texts, essentially fixed by institutional fiat, it also came to mean a body of individuals raised to heaven by the perfection of their lives. In this latter signification, the canon of saints was not closed but open, with new saints always admissible by approved institutional procedures. This distinction is important because in current literary disputes over the canon, both models are sometimes invoked, one on behalf of a relatively fixed canon and the other on behalf of a relatively open one. In any case, our current thinking about canonicity cannot afford to ignore the grounding of the modern term in a history explicitly influenced by Christian institutions. This influence is apparent, for instance, in the way Thomas Carlyle described the heroic figures of literature in 1840:

Nay here in these ages, such as they are, have we not
two mere Poets, if not deified, yet we may say beati-
fied? Shakespeare and Dante are Saints of Poetry:
really, if we think of it, *canonized,* so that it is impiety
to meddle with them. The unguided instinct of the
world, working across all these perverse impediments,
has arrived at such result. Dante and Shakespeare are
a peculiar Two. They dwell apart, in a kind of royal
solitude; none equal, none second to them: in the
general feeling of the world, a certain transcendental-
ism, a glory as of complete perfection, invests these
two. They *are* canonized, though no Pope or Cardi-
nals took a hand in doing it! (Carlyle, 107, emphasis
in original)

At this point we must backtrack a bit to note that *canon* also has
a more purely secular pedigree going back to Alexandrian Greek, in
which the word *kanōn* was used by rhetoricians to refer to a body
of superior texts: *hoi kanōnes* "were the works which the Alexandrian
critics considered as the most perfect models of style and composition, equivalent to our modern term 'The Classics'" (Donnegan).
Exactly how the interplay between the rhetorical and the religious
uses of the notion of *canon* functioned two millennia ago is a matter
well beyond the scope of the present inquiry. What we most need to
learn from the ancient significations of *canon,* however, is that they
ranged in meaning all the way from "a text possessing stylistic virtues
that make it a proper model" to "a text that is a repository of the Law
and the Truth, being the word of God." We should remember also
that the word, as a transitive verb, referred to "a process of inclusion
among the saints."

In the vernacular languages, the meanings of *canon* found in late
Latin were simply extended. In French, for instance, we can find the
following in a modern dictionary: *canon* (1) Gun, barrel of a gun,

cannon; cylinder, pipe, tube; leg (of trousers); and *canon* (2) Canon. *Canon des Écritures*, the sacred canon; *école de droit canon*, school of canon law (Baker). The French is especially useful in reminding us that the word for gun and the word for the law and the sacred texts are simply branches of a single root rather than two totally different words. The fact that in English we regularized separate spellings for the guns and the laws in the later eighteenth century has tended to obscure the common heritage of both of these spellings in the ancient extensions of a word for reed or cane. In English the most relevant meanings of the word *canon* for our purposes are these: A rule, law, or decree of the Church; a general rule, a fundamental principle; the collection or list of the books of the Bible accepted by the Christian Church as genuine and inspired; hence, any set of sacred books; a list of saints acknowledged and canonized by the Church (*OED*).

Guns and ruling are associated in more ways than one. The English, of course, seem particularly responsible for institutionalizing the cane as an instrument for beating docility into subject peoples and Greek into schoolboys. The *OED* illustrates the use of cane as a verb with a quotation from a Victorian newspaper: "I had a little Greek caned into me." Many a native in India had Shakespeare as well as other canonical texts caned into him by the curricular arm of the British Raj. The Empire was based on its cannon, canon, and canes—to a startling degree.

The use of *canon* to mean a body of sacred texts comes to us from Latin rather than Greek, and specifically from the Latin of the Roman Church, where it is an extension of the notion of a canon as rule or law. The most common extension of this sense of the word in literary studies has until very recently been in reference to the works written by any single author. We speak of the Shakespeare canon or the Defoe canon, meaning no more than the works really written by these authors as opposed to those that might be erroneously attributed to them. Inevitably, however, some of the religious connotations of canonicity flow into this secular use. Where there is a canon, there is both power and sanctity. Above all, however, there is discipline. A textual canon is always a disciplinary function. A canon is in every sense a phallocratic object.

First the law, then the sacred texts. As religious practices and beliefs are institutionalized in a church, the canonical texts are separated from the apocrypha, or the angelic from the satanic verses, as matters are put in the Islamic canon. Canonical texts are held to be fully authorized, ultimately attributable to God. They are, therefore, not only sacred but authoritative, truthful. What is excluded from the religious canon turns into mere literature—a principle that we should note, for it says much about literature as a field of study that is not yet a discipline. Perhaps I should at this point make my own position clearer. I have no case to make against either canons or disciplines—in fact the whole thrust of my argument in this book is in favor of making English studies more rather than less disciplined. Disciplines, after all, are the essentials of academic life, and I am an academician. I only want to emphasize that canons and disciplines need one another. They go together. And *discipline*, like *canon*, is a word that scarcely conceals its potential for abuses of power. We need disciplines in order to think productively. We also need to challenge them in order to think creatively.

The tightening of thought that constitutes a discipline is inevitably accompanied by a tightening of control over some canon of texts or methods. For example, as Plato tried to move Greek thought closer to monotheism, he found it necessary to turn Homer into an apocryphal text, a text that tells lies about God. It is clear that Plato and his Socrates admired Homer and knew the Homeric texts the way some Christians know their Bible, but Homer was exposed as literature rather than scripture in Plato's *Republic*—and suffered the consequences. Plato, of course, did not share our concept of literature, which is itself a product of the consolidation of literary study as a branch of aesthetics in the late eighteenth and early nineteenth centuries. What his example illustrates is that the tendency to canon-

methods of study. The study of literature as a discipline (as opposed to the study of Greek and Latin grammar and a mixed bag of classical texts) begins with English works like Lord Kames's *Elements of Criticism* but is really consolidated by the German Romantics in texts like Schiller's *Letters on the Aesthetic Education of Man,* Schelling's *Philosophy of Art* (especially the last section on "The Verbal Arts"), and the section on poetry that closes Hegel's *Aesthetics: Lectures on Fine Art.* In these texts, and in their less systematic English counterparts by Coleridge, Shelley, and others, the notion of literature as a branch of the fine arts, characterized by *Imagination*—the absolutely crucial word—became sufficiently clear and stable to support a field of study.

Literary study, however, has never quite defined its objects as neatly as the sciences have defined theirs. It has hovered between the forms of canonicity proper to science and those proper to religion, sometimes regarding its objects of study as specimens, but more often giving them the status of quasi-religious texts, not grounded in the Word of God, exactly, but in the Imagination, which, as Coleridge so explicitly argues, is analogous to and partakes of the creativity of God the Creator. In making this move, the Romantics and followers like Arnold were actually reversing the Platonic process, putting Literature at the center of culture by claiming that Imagination enabled literary Artists to shape in language or plastic matter versions of Absolute Truth. This Romantic move also resulted in the establishment of canons oriented to a single language and culture, because such canons were felt to embody the Spirit of a particular nation or people. In this manner, English or French or German literature could be seen as a body of material that needed sorting out into canonical and noncanonical texts: those that embodied the proper spirit and those that did not. This sorting, and the exegesis of the chosen texts, accordingly became the projects of a quasi-priestly caste, gradually organized around their national literary canons into academic fields. Our present English departments are, among other things, the inheritors of a field partly organized by this cultural history. They are also partly organized by an older tradition of rhetorical study, which they acquired when they sublated the rhetoric departments in many American universities about a century ago. Rhetoric had been organized around a canon of methods, with texts used merely as examples. English literature organized itself around a canon of texts, relegating the methods of rhetoric to a minor role. The stir and struggle we are now experiencing may indicate that this traditional hierarchy is beginning to become unstable.

In drawing out the connections between canons and forms of institutionalized power, I may have seemed to be headed toward some quasi-Foucaultian critique of power itself, along with a plea for the elimination of all canons. Nothing could be further from my intent, however, for I am persuaded that the connection between institutions and canons is inevitable. Furthermore, our awareness of the existence of canons and our understanding of the processes by which they are maintained and altered makes it possible for us to influence canons through the institutions that support them and to change the institutions through their canons. What I am opposed to is the pretense that there may be some cosmic canon that transcends all institutions because it is based on an unexaminable and unchallengeable Absolute. This, I contend, is the case with notions like Great Books and Western Civ, in which a flock of cultures marches under the banner of a canonical eagle. I also want to suggest that some shifting between canons of texts and canons of methods has been a regular part of cultural history, so that we should regard it as a normal feature of our lives. I believe that we are at a point in cultural and textual studies where a realignment between these two types of canonicity is essential to the health of English studies. At this moment, however, my main point is that there has never been a canon of Great Books.

There is no canon of Great Books, in my view, because there is no intellectual core to the notion of Great Books in the first place. Literary study, though far from being a quantifying science, obtained a degree of coherence by organizing itself around Romantic concepts of Art, Imagination, and Spirit. Other textual studies organize themselves by time, by genre, or by other systems of connection among their objects, just as biology has organized itself around the concepts of life, the cell, and so on. But notions like those of Great Books and Western Civ have no disciplinary focus and hence no academic core. There is, just to consider the most basic matters, absolutely no notion of bookish Greatness that has any coherence whatsoever. Allan Bloom would tell us, I suppose, that all the Great Books exhibit something called Greatness of Soul, but the concept of Great Souls is just as vague—in both adjective and noun—as what it is supposed to define. Nor is the notion of Western Civilization much of an improvement, though Gandhi thought it would be a good idea for the West to attempt it. There can be no notion of textual greatness, I am arguing, apart from a set of texts organized by a discipline. Of course, there have been great philosophers—but only since philosophy has been a discipline could we perceive them as such. Nor is their "greatness" of the same kind as that of Mozart, Shakespeare, or Tintoretto. All these are great only in contexts, partly narrative ones, that allow them to be perceived as such.

Western Civ, I maintain, lacks the coherence for pedagogically sound instruction. Such coherence as it might have, I would add, comes from a philosophy which even its adherents no longer claim to accept. One of the things we need to remember when considering concepts like Western Civ is that they originated in the Eurocentric thinking of German philosophers. The greatest of these, of course, was Hegel, who systematized the notion of cultural progress from East to West in ways that still haunt most of our thinking on these subjects. Let us listen to him a moment:

> The History of the World travels from East to West,
> for Europe is absolutely the end of History, Asia the
> beginning. . . . Although the earth forms a sphere,
> History forms no circle around it, but has on the con-

trary a determinate East, viz., Asia. Here rises the out-
ward physical sun, and in the West it sinks down; here
consentaneously rises the sun of self-consciousness,
which diffuses a nobler brilliance. The History of the
World is the *discipline* of the uncontrolled natural
will, bringing it into obedience to a Universal principle and conferring subjective freedom. The East
knew and to the present day knows only that One is
Free; the Greek and Roman world, that some are free;
the German World knows that All are free. (Hegel,
1956, 103–4, emphasis added)

It would be easy to mock the smug Eurocentrism of Hegelian
thought, but this would involve ignoring some of the complications
and nuances of that thought. In this discussion, however, I intend to
pay more attention to some of the Hegelian nuances that are often
lost in later adaptations of that Eurocentric perspective. What Hegel
meant by the German world, in this instance, was Europe after the
fall of Rome, a Europe that had been overrun by Germanic tribes
moving from east to west: the Angles, the Saxons, the Franks, the
Goths, the Lombards. He also meant a Europe in which ultimately
Protestantism would come to elevate the materialism of the Roman
Catholic Church to a more spiritual level, finally realizing Christ's
message that every human soul is free and worthy of development.
He describes this process, in a memorable passage, as subjecting
Christianity to "the terrible discipline of culture":

Secularity appears now [he was writing of the six-
teenth century] as gaining a consciousness of its in-
trinsic worth—becomes aware of its having a value
of its own in the morality, rectitude, probity and
activity of man. The consciousness of independent
validity is aroused through the restoration of Christian freedom. The Christian principle has now passed

through the terrible discipline of culture, and it first
attains truth and reality through the Reformation.
This third period of the German World extends from
the Reformation to our own times. (Hegel, 1956,
344)

I am introducing Hegel into this discussion of Western Civ and
Great Books for a number of reasons, which I must now try to explain and clarify. As I have already partly indicated, I believe that our
tendency to speak in terms of Western Civ is derived from the degeneration of Hegelian ideas into the repertory of "common sense." I call
this a degeneration because, in this passage from systematic thought
to folk wisdom, Hegel's ideas have been separated from the rationale
that drove them. By putting them back in their Hegelian context, I
hope to show both what they have lost in this transition and how we
shall have to adapt and modify them to make them useful again for
curricular purposes. Let me begin this complex process by pointing
out that for Hegel the idea of studying the West without the East
would be ludicrous. The basic principle involved here is Hegel's view
of history as a dialectical process, in which the new always results
from the negation and sublation of the old, in which certain elements
of the old are retained within the new synthesis. By seeing the West
as the dialectical heir to the East, Hegel incorporates understanding
of the East as a necessary part of the study of Germanic (or Western)
culture. Here is a typical passage in which he specifies the sort of exchange involved in this process:

In the struggle with the Saracens [the Crusades],
European valor had idealized itself to a fair and noble
chivalry. Science and knowledge, especially that of
philosophy, came from the Arabs into the West.
A noble poetry and free imagination were kindled
among the Germans by the East—a fact which directed Goethe's attention to the Orient and occa-

sioned the composition of a string of lyric pearls, in his "Divan," which in warmth and felicity of fancy cannot be surpassed. But the East itself, when by degrees enthusiasm had vanished, sank into the grossest vice. (360)

The East had its time of spiritual flourishing, and sank, as every culture in history is doomed to do, in Hegel's view, until history comes to an end—an end he hoped and believed was being attained in his own time. The fact that history did not end in his time, and that it has taken some surprising turns since then, constitutes part of our problem in putting Hegelian ideas to work today. In terms of Western Civ, however, there are two other aspects of Hegel's thought that we should remember. In recognizing the enduring achievements of the great literary figures of the past, Hegel also insisted on their pastness. In his view the continually increasing distance of the literary past from the present makes the need for a properly modern literature more acute: "No Homer, Sophocles, etc., no Dante, Ariosto, or Shakespeare can appear in our day; what was so magnificently sung, what was so freely expressed, has been expressed; these are materials, ways of looking at them and treating them which have been sung once and for all. Only the present is fresh, the rest is paler and paler" (1975, 608).

Hegel's view of literature is historical through and through. For him, the great texts of the past do not remain enshrined in some timeless heaven of Art but are themselves part of history, valuable as all manifestations of the human spirit are valuable, but becoming paler and paler all the same. The study of literature, if it were undertaken in a Hegelian spirit, would not be a parade of timeless texts but a reading of literary history as the expression of moments in the "discipline of culture." Furthermore, to see literature as properly historical, in Hegel's view, would be to give some privilege to texts that were oppositional or negative in their relation to the prevailing values of their times—which, need I say it, are precisely those texts most often omitted from lists of Great Books and courses in Western Civ. In reminding us that much of art is oppositional, Hegel speaks of the way that certain writers found it necessary to "turn *against* the content that was alone valid hitherto; thus in Greece Aristophanes rose up against his present world, and Lucian against the whole of the Greek past, and in Italy and Spain, when the Middle Ages were closing, Ariosto and Cervantes began to turn against chivalry" (1975, 605, emphasis in original).

For Hegel the whole of Western Civ, the "discipline" of Western culture, is almost unbearable to contemplate. The only thing that redeems this spectacle is the sense that it has a purpose, that it is progressive, because it is the history of Spirit realizing itself through the rise of human consciousness. But we need to catch some echo of his own voice on this matter:

> Without rhetorical exaggeration, a simply truthful combination of the miseries that have overwhelmed the noblest of nations and polities, and the finest exemplars of private virtue—forms a picture of most fearful aspect, and excites emotions of the profoundest and most hopeless sadness, counterbalanced by no consolatory result. We endure in beholding it a mental torture, allowing no defense or escape but the consideration that what has happened could not be otherwise; that it is a fatality which no intervention could alter. And at last we draw back from the intolerable disgust with which these sorrowful reflections threaten us, into the more agreeable environment of our individual life—the Present formed by our private aims and interests. In short we retreat into the selfishness that stands on the quiet shore, and thence enjoys in safety the distant spectacle of

"wrecks confusedly hurled." But even regarding History as the slaughter-bench at which the happiness of peoples, the wisdom of States, and the virtue of individuals have been victimized—the question involuntarily arises—to what principle, to what final aim these enormous sacrifices have been offered. (Hegel, 1956, 21)

Without that final aim, which in Hegel's case is a theological one—that of the Absolute realizing itself through humanity's increasing understanding of the world and the role of Spirit in it—the spectacle of Western Civ is indeed unbearable. What is wrong with our present adaptations of this notion of Western Civ, I am arguing, is that on the one hand they do not acknowledge the horror of the spectacle but present it as a series of glorious achievements, and on the other hand they finesse the question of history itself and of historicism in particular. The past two centuries of historical events have certainly demonstrated that history did not end with Hegel. And surely, philosophical thought during those years has combined with political and social events to make it virtually impossible for us to sustain a Hegelian belief in the direction of history by a providential Absolute.

It will be useful in this context to compare Hegel's view of cultural history as a "slaughter-bench" *(Schlachtbank)*, redeemed only by the progressive domination of Spirit over matter, with Walter Benjamin's view of the same terrain, which is consciously set against the historicism and idealism of Hegel's followers. Benjamin asks "with whom the adherents of historicism actually empathize":

> The answer is inevitable: with the victor. And all rulers are the heirs of those who conquered before them. Hence, empathy with the victor invariably benefits the rulers. Historical materialists know what that means. Whoever has emerged victorious participates to this day in the triumphal procession in which

present rulers step over those who are lying pros-
trate. According to traditional practice, the spoils are
carried along in the procession. They are called cultural treasures, and a historical materialist views them
with cautious detachment. For without exception the
cultural treasures he surveys have an origin which he
cannot contemplate without horror. They owe their
existence not only to the efforts of the great minds
and talents who have created them, but also to the
anonymous toil of their contemporaries. There is no
document of civilization which is not at the same
time a document of barbarism. And just as such a
document is not free of barbarism, barbarism taints
also the manner in which it was transmitted from one
owner to another. A historical materialist therefore
dissociates himself from it as far as possible. He re-
gards it as his task to brush history against the grain.
(Benjamin, 1969, 256–57)

Benjamin, it should be noted, does not deny the greatness of the
minds that have created cultural treasures. Even when trying to speak
as a "historical materialist," he must acknowledge the flashes of Spirit
that animate the treasures of Western Civ—and so, I believe, must
we. But such flashes are not intelligible, not even perceptible, without a context. Hegel's own greatness—and I would be the last to deny
it—can be comprehended, measured, and criticized only in a context of other systematic thinkers. Without the threads of filiation that
bind him to Plato and Aristotle, to Fichte and Schelling, to Marx and
Freud, and above all, without a sense of what dialectic or systematic
thought actually may be, Hegel may only seem, as he did to Goethe's
daughter when he came to dinner, to be "an unclear thinker."

The point I am trying so laboriously to make is that any presentation of Europe's cultural past must itself be laboriously thought

out and carefully presented. When disconnected texts are collected in surveys of Great Books, one of the first things lost is history itself. When texts that speak to one another—that address the same problems, that work in the same medium or genre—are studied, then such courses can make sense. They will make the greatest sense, however, if they take a narrative structure that finally connects them to the present. To return to the example I have been working with, Hegel is important to us because our thought is still shaped by ideas he formulated so powerfully—and because we need to reject some of those ideas (on the actual history of the "Orient," for example) in order to understand our own situation.

In my view, every discipline should offer courses in its own history, or in some coherent segment of that history ending with the present time. But there can be no coherent overview of the historical whole, no single historical core of Great Books embodying something called Western Civilization. And if any single discipline's history were to be privileged as the best embodiment of the ideal that Western Civ fails to reach, that would certainly be the History of Art from Egypt to America, including the powerful influence of African and Oceanian art upon Euro-American modernism—but visual art, like music, is regularly ignored in courses called Western Civ—as if "Civ" were a purely verbal matter. I would privilege sculpture and painting because they are so palpable, so representable, so suited to a generation attuned to visual texts. In the history of art, what my teacher George Kubler called so beautifully "the shape of time" can be grasped as a structure to which other historical events and texts can be attached. However—and here my discourse will take its final turn toward the specific and practical—I also want to argue that historical studies themselves should be preceded or accompanied by another core, designed to help students situate themselves in their own culture, and, in particular, designed to make the basic processes of language itself intelligible and fully available for use. Toward the establishment of such a core I now wish to make the "trivial proposal" mentioned in the title of this chapter.

This proposal will be trivial, perhaps, in the sense that it will make a much smaller claim than that made by Great Books or Western Civ curricula. It will be trivial, however, in another sense: it is an attempt to rethink in modern terms the trivium that was the core of medieval education. This will also be a radical proposal, in that I propose to go back to the roots of our liberal arts tradition and reinstate grammar, dialectic, and rhetoric at the core of college education. These three subjects, you remember, constituted the preliminary studies to the medieval quadrivium of arithmetic, geometry, astronomy, and music. Our culture is too complicated for education to be quadrivial now, but not to accommodate a trivial core. To envision such a thing, we need only rethink what grammar, dialectic, and rhetoric might mean in modern terms. My own rethinking of these terms has taken the form of seeing all three of the trivial arts as matters of textuality, with the English language at the center of them, but noting their extension into media that are only partly linguistic. I offer the results here, with a certain humility, as trivial in yet another sense. This is crude, provisional thinking, meant to stimulate refinements and alternatives rather than to lay down any curricular law.

This modern trivium, like its ancestor, would be organized around a canon of concepts, precepts, and practices rather than a canon of texts. In particular, each trivial study would encourage textual production by students in appropriate modes. Since this is a modern trivium, such production would include, where appropriate, not only speaking and writing but work in other media as well. Similarly, texts for reading, interpretation, and criticism would be drawn from a range of media, ancient and modern. I will present my trivial proposal in the form of a set of courses, each of which would be based not on a canon of sacred texts but on certain crucial concepts to be understood not simply in a theoretical way but in their application to the analysis of specific cultural or textual objects. This means that the specific texts selected could have considerable variety from course to course and place to place, though it may well be that certain texts should prove so useful that they would be widely adopted for use in textual curricula. In some cases, even, "classic" texts from philosophy and literature will present themselves as the most useful things available—which may tell us something about why they have become classics in the first place. At any rate, the specific titles given in the following descriptions are meant to be illustrative rather than prescriptive.

My first trivial topic is grammar, traditionally the driest and narrowest of academic subjects. I propose to change all that by means of a course of study that follows the implications of the grammar of the pronouns all the way to the subject and object positions of discourse. I see grammar, conceived in this generous manner, as an alternative to traditional composition courses, taking perhaps two semesters of work, the first of which might be called Language and Human Subjectivity. The basis of this course would be the way that their mother tongue presents human beings with a set of words and grammatical rules in which they may attain subjectivity at the cost of being subjected. The very heart of such a course would be the grammar of the pronouns, beginning with *I* and *you*, as opposed to *he, she,* and *it*. But this grammar must be connected to the philosophical questions of subject and object and the ethical relationship of *I* and *thou*. The virtual loss of *thou* in English, except in certain religious contexts, would make one point of discussion. In designing such a course I would be careful to use a mixture of theoretical texts and illustrative embodiments of the problems of subjectivity. The necessary theory is conveniently embodied, for instance, in such discussions as those of the linguist Emil Benveniste on "The Nature of Pronouns" and "Subjectivity in Language" (*Problems in General Linguistics,* 1971); in Hegel's dialectic of Master and Servant in the *Phenomenology of Spirit;*

in Freud's *Das Ich und das Es,* which is usually translated as *The Ego and the Id* but which is just as properly translated as *The I and the It;* and in other works by Piaget, Vygotsky, and Lacan, for example.

Some of this is not easy reading, I will grant you, but basic college work in the sciences is not easy either. There is no reason why we should not ask students to make an effort in the study of human textuality that is comparable to what they would make in economics, biology, or any other discipline. On the other hand, we have the opportunity—and the necessity, I would say—of also presenting our topic through texts that embody the charms of specificity and narrativity. In the present instance, my colleagues (in Brown University's Department of Modern Culture and Media) and I have found that the cases of "wild" children—such as the boy found in Aveyron in the eighteenth century, whose case is available in print and in François Truffaut's excellent film on the subject—make these issues concrete and emotionally engaging. (See Lucien Malson, *Wolf Children and the Problem of Human Nature,* 1972, which includes a full translation of Itard's *The Wild Boy of Aveyron;* and Roger Shattuck, *The Forbidden Experiment: The Story of the Wild Boy of Aveyron,* 1980.) Another extremely useful narrative approach to these matters is embodied in Samuel Delany's *Babel-17* (1976), a work of science fiction focused on a language that is dehumanizing precisely because it lacks the pronouns *I* and *you.*

Other matters that properly belong to a course on Language and Human Subjectivity would include the problem of human alienation (Hegel and Marx) and the very specific problems of feminine subjectivity in language, especially those relating to the loss of women's family names in history through the adoption of husband's names by wives, and to the use of the male pronoun as the general pronoun for males and females. This topic is clearly presented Dale Spender's *Man Made Language* (1980) and many other works. The whole question of style and personal voice in writing can also be properly deployed under this rubric, along with the study of the essay and the lyric poem as literary forms that have for several centuries enacted the problems of attaining subjectivity in language. Here also is the place for students to experiment as writers with the subjective modes of textuality. Many traditional dimensions of the English curriculum can find their places in such a course as this, and they will be energized in the process by their functioning in a course with the specific conceptual goal of developing students' awareness of the relation between language and human subjectivity.

The second semester of "grammatical" study in my new trivium would treat the topic of Representation and Objectivity. Representation is an activity in which a textual subject positions someone or something else as a textual object. The growth of the sciences in modern Europe and America is a process elaborately connected to the development of "objective" discourses. One could almost define science as an objective discourse about a certain body of material. Because of the importance and power of such discourses it is essential for students to learn how they work and what their strengths, costs, and limitations may be. The problems of representation and objectification become especially important in those disciplines involving objects of study that have a strong claim to a subjectivity that may be suppressed (even violently) in order to represent them as objects. It is in the human or social sciences, then, that we will find the most suitable textual material for a course like this one: sociology, anthropology, and history will offer us topics that are at least accessible to our competences if not within them.

A semester's work in Representation and Objectivity should share some theory with the study of subjectivity in language, but it should also have a theoretical base of its own in theories of representation and narrativity, whether semiotic or New Historicist. It should also draw upon the self-reflective meta-discourse of whatever field is selected for emphasis in a particular version of the course. That is, if the course takes anthropological writing as its focus, it should include both samples of unreflective anthropologizing and works that stand in a meta-discursive relation to such unreflective work, such as selections from Lévi-Strauss's *Tristes Tropiques* (1970) and writing on the problems of anthropological discourse by Clifford Geertz and James Clifford. If a historical topic is to be the center of the course, meta-historical work by Charles Collingwood, E. H. Carr, and Hayden White might compose part of the theoretical basis of the investigation. It is also easy to imagine a course focused on European representations of its Oriental Other, which takes Edward Said's *Orientalism* as a point of departure. No meta-text should be awarded a position of unquestioned validity, but each should be used to open up the questions of objectivity and representation so that students can enter them as writers. I think the best results will come in courses with a clear focus, such as the anthropologizing of Native Americans, or the historicizing of a specific event in American life, or the sociologizing of a specific American class or culture. In studying such a topic, a range of objective and frankly subjective discourses, as well as meta-discourses, would function as ways of learning both about the specific topic and about the larger processes of representation and objectification that enable scientific discourses to function.

The second trivial topic in the core curriculum I am proposing would be dialectic. In its modern dress, and because the word *dialectic* has drifted far from its earlier usage, a course in this trivial topic might be called System and Dialectic. Such a course would have as its object of study discourses that work at a high level of abstraction and systematization, in which texts are constructed not so much by representing objects as by abstracting from them their essential qualities or their principles of composition. This is preeminently the domain of philosophy itself, and especially of the tradition of Continental philosophy from the pre-Socratics to Derrida. It may well be that literature departments would need help from their friends in philosophy to mount courses that approach this topic effectively, but several decades of literary theory ought to have made them readier to undertake such a project themselves than they were some years ago.

The intent of such study would be, in part, to make available to students the tradition of clear and systematic thinking that has been so crucial to the history of what Richard Rorty has called "the rich North Atlantic nations"—so that such students may learn to employ the resources of logic and dialectic in their own thinking and writing. A further intent, however, would be to introduce students to those countertrends, arising mainly within philosophy itself, that seek to criticize or even undo that very tradition. Put more specifically, such absolutely essential philosophers as Plato, Aristotle, Kant, and Hegel might be read and discussed in speech and writing, along with such antithetical writers as Nietzsche, Wittgenstein, Heidegger, Derrida, Rorty, and Davidson. Such a course might have a particular theme, such as philosophies of science, which would bring Aristotle, Bacon, Locke, Kuhn, and Feyerabend into prominence, or government, which would make Plato, Machiavelli, Hobbes, Montesquieu, and others important—or education, or language, or justice, or freedom. The point would be for students to learn both how to use and how to criticize discourse that takes reason, system, and logical coherence as its principles of articulation.

The last of the trivial topics I am proposing might well be taught first in any sequence of core courses, because it deals with more familiar matters and perhaps even with more immediately accessible material. I am not offering a rigid order or sequence of courses here, in any case, but trying to suggest how one might go about revitalizing the old trivium, the third division of which, you will remember, was rhetoric. I would be inclined to call a modern course in rhetoric something like Persuasion and Mediation. Such a course would obviously include the traditional arts of manipulation of audiences but would also point toward the capacities and limits of the newer media, especially those that mix verbal and visual textuality to generate effects of unprecedented power. Such a course would embrace the traditional topics of rhetoric but would extend them in certain specific directions. One might well wish to begin with Aristotle's

Rhetoric, but in this kind of course the *Poetics* would also have a place as a discussion of both another type of manipulation and a specific medium (tragic drama) that mediates human experience in a particular way, incorporating the hegemonic codes of a particular cultural situation. From here one might go on to Nietzsche's *Birth of Tragedy* and Brecht on "Epic Theatre." In this connection it would be especially effective to move from the rhetoric of theater to the rhetoric of film and visual spectatorship in general, in which the gendering of subjects and objects of viewing could be considered (as in Laura Mulvey, Teresa de Lauretis, and John Berger, for instance), along with other ideological analyses of the rhetoric of the mass media in both direct (overt) and indirect (covert) manipulation of viewers. Plays, films, and television texts would be the objects of rhetorical analysis in such a course, along with such more overtly persuasive texts as political speeches and advertisements.

In such a curricular core of study, students might well encounter as many "classic" texts as in more traditional core curricula, but these texts would not be studied simply "because they are there" but rather as the means to an end of greater mastery of cultural processes by the students themselves. By putting language and textuality at the center of education, we would not be making some gesture of piety toward the medieval roots of education, but we would certainly be acknowledging the cultural past of our institutions. More important, however, we would be responding to the "linguistic turn" of so much of modern thought and to the media saturation that is the condition of our students' lives as well as of our own. Already, in such a trivium, the cultural past will have begun to be presented as a body of texts that can help students to understand their current cultural situation—just as they help their teachers (who also, of course, continue to be students). This trivium should serve, as well, to whet the appetite for other courses that attend more specifically to the historical narratives of one or another mode of cultural activity. If the pigs and the dogs learn to communicate and negotiate with one another, perhaps they can turn this flock of cultures into a nest of singing birds, and make such music as will stir the corrupting carcass of Western Civilization itself. That, at least, is my hope. But now it is time to shift the focus from general education back to the possibility of a discipline called English.

assignment 4

Pacesetter English

For the past several years I have been working with a group of dedicated teachers from secondary schools, colleges, and universities, along with representatives of the College Board and the Educational Testing Service, to develop an alternative English course for all high school students. My involvement began when I was asked to chair the task force that would set the guidelines for the English version of Pacesetter, the College Board's new program to improve high school teaching in mathematics, Spanish, and English. Eventually, Bill McBride of Colorado State University and I cochaired the Pacesetter English task force. We spent two years discussing and debating the merits of various possibilities for changing the way English is taught in high schools. Our problem was initially presented in the form of providing an alternative to current courses for the twelfth and final year of formal schooling.

As cochairman, I made it my business to get all the possible alternatives on the table, including the possibility of basing the whole course on Shakespeare. Coming, as I did, from what is perceived as an elite university, I felt myself in no position to tell high school teachers what to do. As things developed, however, it became clear that I had been invited to do this job because my ideas on teaching English, including some now presented in this book, had come to the attention of both the organizers of the program and the teachers on the task force. What was wanted was a course that would help students to gain what I had called "textual power." It was as if

I had been told (though no one ever said it directly), "You've had a lot to say about how English should be taught. Here is your chance to put up or shut up. Help us come up with a better course in senior (or junior) English for high school students—or slink back to your ivy tower and stop pontificating."

It is not easy to stop pontificating. And the challenge was irresistible. So I set to work. When the task force had finished laying down its guidelines, I moved on to assist the groups of high school teachers and testing experts devising a yearlong syllabus, with portfolios and various kinds of exercises and assessments. And when we were finished with that, I continued to work with these groups, playing a small role in staff-development courses for teachers who would field-test the course—helping to design common assessments, to revise the course in response to reports from the field, and so on. I am still involved as deeply as I can be. And I want to say that I have never spent time with a group of people more creative, more dedicated, and more fun to work with. What follows here is a brief overview of the course. I wrote it when we first completed a version of Pacesetter English, and have revised it as the course itself has developed. After the overview, I will offer a brief report on the current status of the course.

PREAMBLE: "VOICES OF MODERN CULTURES"

By their final years, most secondary school students have been taking courses in English or language arts for a dozen years. Pacesetter English is a serious attempt to provide a suitable capstone course for all those years of study—for students who expect to enter the workforce when they graduate and for those who plan to continue their formal education in college, recognizing that both those expectations are subject to change. A capstone course in English should enable students to use all they have learned in their previous years of study, and it should help them to realize how that learning connects to the lives they hope to live. The goal of such a course should be for all students to attain the highest degree of literacy that they can.

Literacy involves the ability to understand and to produce a wide variety of texts that use the English language—including work in the traditional literary forms, in the practical and persuasive forms, and in the modern media as well. Whether students go on to higher education or enter the workforce after graduation, their success will depend to a great extent on their ability to understand and use the English language. That is why this course makes language itself—and its use in various forms, genres, and media—the center of attention.

Language can be as personal as the pronouns *I* and *you*—or as impersonal as a tax form. To live as mature human beings and functioning members of society we need to be able to communicate with others. In some cultures the ability to speak and listen carries the whole burden of communication. But our culture is organized by the most complex system of textuality the world has ever known. We need speaking and listening skills, to be sure, and we need to be literate in the traditional sense: able to read and write. But we also need to be "literate" across a various and complex network of different kinds of writing and various media of communication.

It is this complexity that has led us to the use of the word *text* in designing the Pacesetter English course. Poems, plays, stories, letters, essays, interviews, books, magazines, newspapers, movies, television shows, yes, and even tax forms, are all different kinds of texts. What the course aims at, then, is to increase the textual power of the students who take it: to help them learn how to read in the fullest sense of that word. Reading, in this sense of the word, means being able to place or situate a text, to understand it from the inside, sympathetically, and to step away from it and see it from the outside, critically.

It means being able to see a text for what it is and to ask also how it connects—or fails to connect—to the life and times of the reader.

This is textual power, but textual power does not stop there; it also includes the ability to respond, to talk back, to write back, to analyze, to extend, to take one's own textual position in relation to Shakespeare—or to any kind of text. Shakespeare wants audiences whose love of language and ability to respond to it matches his own textual power. A tax form (like most other bureaucratic forms) wants a person who can follow directions. Every text offers its audience a certain role to play. Textual power involves the ability to play many roles—and to know that one is playing them—as well as the ability to generate new texts, to make something that did not exist before somebody made it. That—all that—is what this course is about.

The course is also—as its title proclaims—about "voices" and "cultures." Modern American culture is a product of its history—a history in which many voices have spoken and continue to be heard: voices from our past, voices from abroad, individual voices, institutional voices, the loud voice of the media and the still, small voice of individual conscience. This course is about listening to those voices, understanding how one culture can be made out of many voices, and finding the voices one needs to express oneself and be heard in the midst of this hubbub. This notion of *voice*, of course, is a metaphor drawn from speech—and this course will not neglect the skills of speaking and listening, but it will also stress the ability to understand and use the written word, and it will offer at least an introduction to the languages of the modern media. But let us look at the course in more detail and see how these ideas will work in action.

THE COURSE

The common features of the course as it is taught in different schools should not be a particular set of works to be "covered" but a set of certain kinds of works to be studied and responded to in certain ways. That is, the emphasis must be on the students' ability to situate and comprehend a range of texts in different genres and media, from different times and places, and to produce new texts of their own in response to what they have read and considered. In order to make the intent of the course concrete, it will be described here in terms of specific works and projects, but we will also offer for every unit a set of criteria that should enable substitutions to suit local conditions.

In any case, all the texts considered in the course, from the past and the present, from far away and from close to home, should be studied in such a way as to connect them to the issues and concerns of this country and its people at the present time. A play by Shakespeare chosen for this course, for example, should be studied both as a voice from another culture, another time, and as a voice that addresses human concerns that are still important and alive for us. That, too, will become clearer as we make a brief tour through the six units that constitute Pacesetter English.

THE UNITS
Unit 1. Introduction to "Voices of Modern Cultures"

At the center of this unit is the student, and that student's relation to language. Students will be asked to consider their own position as cultured speakers, with voices shaped by their heritages, their experiences, and their schooling. If this were *Sesame Street,* we might say that this unit is brought to its audience by the pronouns *I, you,* and *we.* Each student will be asked to investigate how she or he is "situated" as an individual who belongs to certain groups and addresses insiders and outsiders in different voices. Students will be asked to consider their present command of language and voices, invited to take pride in what they know, and encouraged to strive to increase their linguistic range and depth.

At the same time, they will be investigating the voices of a range of writers addressing the questions "Who am I?" and "Who are we?" For this purpose, lyric poems and essays will provide the most useful examples of linguistic grace and power in the service of personal expression and self-examination. The whole purpose of Pacesetter English and its relation to traditional English courses can be found here in Unit 1. Like traditional courses, it will present poems and essays to be read by students. But it will present these texts as examples of textual power for students to emulate. The goal will be for students to see themselves as users of language, with voices of their own that are similar to those of the writers they are reading. Confronting the same kinds of questions and concerns as those writers, students can see themselves as active partners in the writing process. In this mode, they should read not only to understand but also to emulate the text they are reading. "What can I learn from this text, this writer, about how to express myself?" is a question that energizes the relationship of the student as reader to the text being read. It is this energy that should drive this whole course.

Unit 2. "Stranger in the Village": Encountering the Other, Being the Other

The pronoun *they* dominates this unit, which is about the way culture and language work to include and exclude individuals, but the pronouns *I* and *we* are back again, too, since the unit is about I-they or us-them relationships. Essays and stories about the situation of being an "other" —a stranger in a village—or about encountering such a stranger will make the core readings for this unit. And once again, students will be reading these texts in preparation for writing their own narratives about such an encounter. The experiences of James Baldwin in a Swiss village or George Orwell in a Burmese town (or comparable texts) will be read not only as "literature" but also as "writing"—as solutions to the same kind of task that the students themselves will be performing. The difference between this kind of reading and traditional reading might be thought of as comparable to the difference between just watching a play or a basketball game and watching one in order to learn some moves you might make yourself on stage or on the court. The goal of the unit is to help students avoid feeling like strangers in the village of literature but to feel instead like members of a literary culture that includes them as well as writers like Baldwin and Orwell.

Unit 3. Cultures and Voices in a Single Text

In this unit students will explore the power of a single complex text (such as a novel) to represent a medley of voices engaged in a conversation and/or a struggle for cultural space. This unit should resemble study of the novel as it is presently undertaken in senior English classes. (This course, after all, is not being written on a blank slate but is a development of the best practice currently available.) But for Pacesetter, this study of a novel will be different in certain crucial respects. First of all, the novel must be chosen not simply because it has literary merit but because—in addition to literary merit—it takes up directly the problem of voices speaking from places separated by cultural gaps. (This is a theme that will return in the other units as well.) In this unit "voice" will be considered specifically as dialect and register, speech patterns that are audible or visible signs of the groups that use them—signs of class, signs of race, signs of gender, signs of educational level.

This is, in a certain sense, hot stuff. We are all sensitive to the ways in which our language marks us, enables—or disables—us in certain situations. As a country, we do not like to think of ourselves as divided into distinct classes by our speech. We attribute that kind of thing to the English. And perhaps our social classes are not so distinct as theirs. But we are not exactly a melting pot, either. Language, with its textual power to enable or disable us, is always at work in the ways we speak and write.

The purpose of this unit is to look at language working in a fictional situation that is recognizably American but in which different varieties of the American language are represented. In considering the voices within this text, students will be encouraged to "situate" the different voices. There is no voice without a group—and that group's culture—behind it. To situate in this sense is to "place" a dialect or register, to ask who speaks it, where they come from, and which of the values they share are embodied in their speech.

In studying a novel, one asks about the voice or voices in which the narrative is told: Who is speaking to us? What kind of voice is that? Does it present itself as reliable, trustworthy? How does it establish its authority? How does that voice compare to the voices of characters as they are represented? Is the narrator a character? Is the narrator the author? When is each voice at its most eloquent pitch? What are its strengths? When does that voice reach limits or barriers? Do characters speak always in one voice, or in more than one? How do different characters speak to one another?

The length of a novel requires prolonged engagement with it by the class. One needs time to read it, time to discuss it, time to write responses to it. In this unit, the novel chosen should not be a fantastic work but one set in a time and place that is accessible by means of other texts. The novel, too, should be seen as a voice speaking from a particular cultural site. Knowing more about the author, more about the background of the represented world, should enable students to read a text more powerfully. The point is not to find the answers to fictional questions in the author's life or in the history of a time and place but rather to use such information to ask more interesting questions about that novel. A novel that is about a known spot in the world is also always an interpretation of that spot and that world. It is a text, a voice, speaking about a place as it looks from a certain spot.

In this unit one can hardly expect students to emulate the author by writing a novel, but one can expect them to understand that novels are made by human beings with ideas and feelings, strengths and weaknesses, axes to grind and values to promote. The point of the unit is to help students develop their ability to read a text as coming from some specific source, a human being inhabiting a particular cultural place—and to ask how the fictional events and characters represented in that printed text connect to their own lives, their own hopes and fears, their own values and beliefs. A good novel should help us understand more about some other place or time—but it should also bring us to a deeper knowledge of ourselves and our own place and time. One reason for studying the voices in a novel is to listen for echoes of the voices that will become ours when we assert our own textual powers.

Unit 4. Inheriting Earlier Voices

This is meant to be a major unit (planned to cover eight weeks of the course) in which a dramatic text from the past is the center of an investigation that has two parts or tracks. One of these tracks has to do with the double situation of any work from the past—in its own time and in ours. The other has to do with the spoken voice and theatrical production. Neither of these tracks is simple. In a course that is built around the metaphor of voice and the concept of culture, this unit is the centerpiece around which everything else turns. We have chosen a play by Shakespeare for this model version of the course not simply because of his famous name but because of his expressive mastery of spoken English. To speak his lines with understanding is to enrich one's own ability to use the medium of spoken English and, ultimately, one's ability to listen, read, write as well.

We have also chosen a play, *Othello,* in which the issues of cultural conflict are in the foreground. Othello himself is a stranger, not in a village but in one of the great city states of his time, Venice. In the play Shakespeare himself has made racial and gender differences the pivots on which the tragedy turns. It is also a play about reason and emotion, about evidence and argument, about truthfulness and deceit. And finally, because it is a play written four centuries away from our own time, with a history of productions and performances, it offers an opportunity to consider performance as interpretation, performances as "readings" of the play, readings that changed over time to suit different audiences in different cultures. The simple question of whether the role of this dark-skinned Moor would be played by a black man or by a white man in blackface—or whether Desdemona would be played by a woman or a boy—turns out not to have been so simple in certain times and places.

One track of this unit, then, will give attention to situating the play in the history of its writing and its productions down to the present time. Another track will involve thinking about it as theater, as staging, as vocal interpretation and performance. The idea, here, is to get students thinking about the play the way a director must think about staging it, the way an actor must think about expressing character, not just through the voice, but through the body and its movements as well. This means giving students the opportunity to put on scenes from the play themselves, to view different performances on video, to discuss and write about the play not simply as a written text but as the basis for many possible realizations. To read a play knowing that you may direct or act in a scene from it is to read actively, as a participant. One project in this unit should be the keeping of an actor's or director's notebook, so that the student reads the play looking for keys to the way a scene should be dramatized or a role should be acted.

Literature, Ezra Pound once said, is news that stays news. That is true enough, but it is also true that readers must help to renew literary texts by connecting them to their own times, their own lives. Thinking about the modern performance of a play from another time, another culture, makes all these questions of interpretation real and vital, offers the student, once again, the chance to be not the passive recipient of literature but an active participant, the partner of the writer in the realization of a text.

Unit 5. Film, Language, and Culture

One of the most powerful voices in modern culture is that of film. It is an international medium, but unlike the play or the novel, it is one in which this country has played a decisive role from its beginnings a century ago to the present time. Like the drama, film uses spoken language, but films have never been merely recordings of plays. They are a medium to which speech, music, and sound effects all contribute, but the medium is primarily visual. The composer Richard Wagner said that he wanted each of his operas to be a *Gesamtkunstwerk*—a total work of art. Film often comes close to achieving that. But to understand film is to realize that it is dominated by its apparatus—by the camera and the editing table in particular.

The goal of this unit is to enable students to "read" films with a real grasp of the language of the medium. To achieve this we propose studying one film as a sort of laboratory example of how the apparatus works to achieve its effects. In our model syllabus we have used a film by Alfred Hitchcock for this purpose, because Hitchcock is a cinema magician whose tricks are so powerful that they reveal themselves easily to an attentive "reader." Studying such a film will be the occasion for students to learn how the apparatus works. One project associated with part of the unit will be the student's own "storyboard" or "shot list" of a film or video. That is, students, working in small groups, perhaps, will either demonstrate how one might film a scene of their own choosing, or they will use the same technique to analyze a scene from a film, a television commercial, or any other appropriate text.

Another very useful possibility for this part of the unit would be a film by Orson Welles, especially his version of *Othello,* which is very definitely a film based on Shakespeare rather than a recording of a stage performance. Even if not studied in depth, this film would make an excellent transition from a drama unit based on *Othello* to this film unit. Like Hitchcock, and like certain Impressionist painters, Welles makes the viewer very aware of the medium itself, even while using it to represent its objects with great power and eloquence.

Once again, the idea in this unit is to help students learn how the medium works from the inside, to become better readers by gaining a deeper understanding of how certain texts are composed. The second film selected for this unit should be one in which the larger themes of the course are represented: voices in cultural conflict or conversation. One example that we have proposed is a late Western film by John Ford, *The Man Who Shot Liberty Valance.* This film is a good example of cultural conflict and conversation because it is about two cultures that come into conflict: the old West and the new. It is also about how the media, and journalism in particular, deal with truth and legend. It also offers representations of women and of ethnic minorities, including a freed slave, Pompey, coming to terms with the positions offered them in the culture of the American West. There is much food for thought in this film, which even gives us two different versions of the same crucial event, leaving us very much aware of the difficult gap between any event and the cultural representation of it.

In discussing this cinematic text (or an equivalent), students should be expected to put their knowledge of the film apparatus to work as they analyze how this film uses the resources of the medium to generate responses from its viewers and to make its own points about the world that it represents, just as they would consider the resources of language in reading a poem or a persuasive essay. A good understanding of how films work should help students to a better understanding of how written texts use resources that are in certain ways very similar but often crucially different. In Hitchcock's film *Psycho,* for example, a shot of Norman Bates from below, against a background of stuffed birds of prey, works much the way a verbal metaphor works. This is a course in which all the units should connect to one another and reinforce one another, with the constant goal being greater awareness of language and greater textual power for the student.

Unit 6. Mediating Culture/The Representation
of Events and People

At the center of this unit is the study of those textual· media that represent culture for us and thus influence the culture itself: especially print and video journalism, but not excluding personal accounts and oral histories. The idea driving this unit is that students should understand the news media as always offering not transparent reflections on events and people but interpretations of these things, presented with varying degrees of reliability and power. To distinguish power from reliability will be a major function of this unit. The point is not to pretend to offer students some magic talisman that will enable them to tell truth from falsehood in the media but rather to help them understand "mediation" (the pouring of raw data through the sieve of any particular medium) as a textual process that requires interpretation.

As the culminating unit of the course, this one should lead to a serious piece of work on the way that an event or a group has been represented in one or more media. This work should also include the students' own representation or mediation of this material. As in other units, here students will be examining the way that this kind of textual job has been done—and they will be doing the job themselves. For the unit to work the instructor must make a good choice about the central "event" or "problem in representation" to be studied—something important enough to have been reported on and mediated in different ways in different places. We think that ideally it should be an event or problem situated somewhat in the past but not so far back in time that there will not be people who remember it and can talk about it. We also think that this is an occasion to select an event that was important to the people living in the part of the country where the course is being taught. It might be a national event with local impact, or a local event of importance. But it should be something substantial enough to have received many kinds of coverage and responses.

Ideally, this study should cross several media covering the same event, but if time or the availability of materials makes this difficult, different representations within a single medium should be studied—such as different newspapers or different television stations reporting the same event. Another idea would be to compare media coverage with reports from individuals who participated in or remember the event or problem being investigated. This study should conclude with a balanced appraisal of the strengths and weaknesses of different representations—and with each student's own perspective on the event or problem and the reporting or representing of that material. The whole point of this kind of study is for students to learn how an event that took place in the past is connected to their present lives, and how the various media of representation offer different versions of that event—how, even in a single medium, such as print journalism, different newspapers may offer quite different versions of the same event.

The function of this unit is to enable students to refine their sense of how events are investigated and reported, both by studying an example of reporting and by producing an investigative text of their own. If the unit works properly, they will be reading as reporters and writing as readers. That is, they will always position themselves both inside and outside the texts they are considering. This is meant to be a substantial unit, with time for them to produce the final major item for their portfolios.

WHAT SHOULD STUDENTS HAVE LEARNED FROM THIS COURSE?

Like all English courses, this one should lead to better reading and writing skills, but in this case it should also lead to a better understanding of how each student is situated in our textualized, mediated world. That is, we hope that students completing this course will not only read and write better but will understand how reading and writing connect to film and television—and how they themselves can become better and more critical consumers of all the texts and media they encounter. Students assembling and reviewing their portfolios should be asking themselves, "What voices can I understand? What voices can I use? And what do my voices have to do with who I am and what I can be?" These are the questions that students should be addressing in the last month of this course. What we hope for the students who have taken this course is that they will be able to say that they have increased their ability to handle many American voices—without having been cut off from the voices of their parents, their past, their heritage. The promise of this country, expressed in its motto in a foreign language—*e pluribus unum,* from many one— is the promise that one nation and one people can be made out of individuals coming from all over the world, in all sorts of conditions of life. The purpose of this course is to help students recognize and use the many voices out of which the one nation and its culture are always being made and remade.

It is too early to judge just what impact this course will have on American education, because that depends upon how widely it is adopted and how well the logistics of national assessment can be accomplished. But it is very clear already that the course itself is being well received. Comments about Pacesetter English from teachers and students have been very encouraging. In the academic year 1995– 96, 178 teachers and 7,280 students were involved in these courses in places ranging from Miami to San Jose. For 1996–97, more than 400 teachers and 21,000 students were scheduled to use the program. There are massive economic and social problems facing American education, which no curriculum can solve by itself. But even in a bad situation, it helps to have a curriculum that both students and teachers can believe in, because they can see that it is aimed at helping students to develop better intellectual equipment for the lives they are actually living and will continue to live.

CHAPTER FIVE

A Fortunate Fall?

Eftsoon so too will our own sphoenix spark spirt his
spyre and sunward stride the rampant flambe. Ay,
already the sombrer opacities of the gloom are sphanished! Brave footsore Haun! Work your progress!
Hold to! Now! Win out, ye divil ye! The silent
cock shall crow at last. The west shall shake the east
awake. Walk while ye have the night for morn, light-
breakfastbringer, morroweth whereon every past shall
full fost sleep. Amain.

                                        —Joyce, Finnegans Wake

The concept of a fortunate fall, the *felix culpa* of
Medieval Christian thought, in which the original
sin of Adam and Eve was seen as fortunate because
it led to the Redeemer, was modernized by James
Joyce early in *Finnegans Wake* as a *foenix culprit*
(23), a guilty figure rising like a phoenix from the ashes of its funeral
pyre, perpetually, without redemption, like Finnegan at his wake,
Finn again and again. In the later passage from same book quoted
as the epigraph to this chapter, the phoenix has metamorphosed into
a Westernized Sphinx, a version of Hegel's Germanic culture, con-
taminated, perhaps, by Nietzsche's blond beast (Haun/Hun), that
has triumphed over the dark Mediterranean power of Spain (sombrer . . . sphanished) in the name of progress, and is now poised,
in its own darkness, "to shake the east awake." We could continue
unpacking the layers of meaning in this text—this creature of darkness (Haun, divil) seems to be impregnating the east with his phallic
church spires and enlisting it into his footsore progress—but my in-

tention here is not to explicate Joyce's text but to use his splendid language as a way of thinking about the problem of English studies at the present time. For the field of English, as I have tried to demonstrate in earlier chapters, has been powerfully connected both to the Hegelian concept of history as a progress toward absolute knowledge and to the imperial projects of England and the United States. Which means that the awakening of the East—and the South— which is also called multiculturalism, may cause English as we have known it to be "sphanished" as well.

As I see it, the many possible fates of English can be clarified by seeing them in terms of two possible directions in which English as a field of study might go. One of them came up in a conversation I had recently with a graduate student who remembered a former teacher saying, "English may go the way of Classics—and it can't happen soon enough." Which means, as I interpret it, that the speaker, and others of his persuasion, would like to see English as a small, elite field of study, devoted to the past, and without responsibilities for general education or the teaching of writing. No "service courses," no uninterested students fulfilling requirements, just dedicated scholars and students who want to emulate them in pursuit of a humanistic education that is its own reward. One can see the beauty of it, for those privileged enough to partake of such intellectual pleasures, but Tennyson's "Lotos-Eaters" come to mind. (Even Tennyson has his intellectual uses—I should be the last to deny it. My afternoons spent mooning over his pages were not entirely wasted.) Still, if the field of English were to become such an elite preserve, much of the work of English would still remain to be done—and perhaps that foenix culprit Rhetoric would arise again to undertake the work.

The second direction, the other way to go, would be for English faculties to rethink their enterprise as a discipline—that is, to construct a discipline out of what has been merely a field, organized, like a burial ground, around the textual tombs of the great dead, with particular acolytes pronouncing elegies over the most prominent monuments. I shall not pursue this metaphor, which was explored so richly in the context of French literary study by Jean-Paul Sartre half a century ago (Sartre, 22–28), except to say that I am not going to propose that we desecrate the tombs and liquidate the elegists. If we can reconstruct this field as a productive discipline, there will be places aplenty for the great English texts—but not for monuments, because the texts that still speak to us are not dead. The question is, how can we begin, in the midst of our difficulties and squabbles, to reconstruct our field as a discipline. My answer, to put it in grossly oversimplified form, is to replace the canon of texts with a canon of methods—to put a modern equivalent of the medieval trivium at the center of an English education. I have already presented this "trivial proposal" in Chapter 4, in terms of what English departments might contribute to general education, but I also would like it understood that such a core of courses would make a superb preparation for a concentration or major in the discipline of English. In this, my final chapter, I will try to clarify what I mean by reorienting English from a field to a discipline, and then I will address some of the practical problems faced by English departments at the present time.

English as a Discipline

As a field of study in the United States, English has been organized around the literary history of England and America. Other Anglophone literatures—even Canadian—have held, at best, a peripheral place in this organization. And somewhere near the center, but almost obscured now, lies a philological organization of the field in terms of the history of the English language, from the Anglo-Saxon of the first Germanic invaders of the British Isles, through the Middle English that developed from a mixture of Anglo-Saxon and Norman French after 1066, to the more modern modes of the language, including the one canonized as the "American Language" by H. L. Mencken in the first half of the twentieth century. In practice the field is organized in the form of survey courses—usually separate surveys of British and American literature—arranged chronologically, plus courses in literary periods or major authors, often supported by requirements for English majors to study texts from earlier periods. The ideal English major emerges from this program of study in possession of a thin but clear sense of English and American literary history as a narrative (the Story of English), with some periodizing concepts (Renaissance, Romanticism, and so on), and with a somewhat deeper knowledge of a few authors and texts. The average English major graduates with an even thinner and muddier command of this narrative: that "little learning" which Alexander Pope believed was worse than none.

English majors these days all learn some critical concepts and perhaps a bit of literary theory, but if you ask them what makes any particular text a work of "literature," you will rarely get a satisfactory response. If it's in the courses, it's literature, if not, not—which is pretty much the way Roland Barthes dealt with this question some decades ago. English majors generally write better than other students, and one hopes that their studies had something to do with this. There is no reason to think it didn't, but most English majors chose the field because reading and writing came easily to them in the first place. I am suggesting that the way our present configuration of the English curriculum plays out in practice is discouraging, even dispiriting. English departments are not doing the old job very well, leaving aside the question of whether it is the right job to be doing. When I have seen the job done about as well as possible, as in the old English Semester at the University of Iowa, it has left me feeling that we might have given our students something more worthy of the splendid efforts they had made. My response to this feeling has been almost three decades spent trying to envision the old field of English reconstructed as a discipline of textuality.

What I mean by a discipline of textuality has been adumbrated in the previous chapters and assignments, but now is the time to organize those scattered glimpses into something more systematic. I would like this discussion to be practical enough for actual attempts to embody it in programs, yet not so specific as to suggest that there is only one right way to undertake the project. To that end, rather than speaking in terms of courses and reading lists, I will present the elements of the discipline under four distinct though overlapping headings: theory, history, production, and consumption. These may well be studied in courses that emphasize one or another, but they can never be isolated, one from the other. My basic assumption here is that these four elements of textuality deserve roughly equal weight in the organization of the discipline, though I see theory as constituting the disciplinary core.

Theory

By theory I mean a canon of methods to be used in studying the other three aspects of textuality: how to situate a text (history), how to compose one (production), and how to read one (consumption). Theory, which has existed since ancient times, now consists of grammar, rhetoric, dialectic, poetics, hermeneutics, semiotics, grammatology, and other modes of understanding textuality. If English is to be a discipline, theory must be at the center of our teaching. We learned — or should have learned — something like this from Northrop Frye more than forty years ago, and I must acknowledge, here as elsewhere, my great debt to him. But for Frye, theory was still in the service of an aesthetic project, a form of poetics. My project is more rhetorical, with textuality, rather than literature, as its principal object. And I have argued, here as elsewhere, that this shift is crucial to any reconstruction of the discipline. Putting theory at the center of our discipline, however — even theories of textuality — does not mean treating works of theory as we are used to treating literary texts. It would be easy to turn the study of theory into a set of Great Theories, Great Theoreticians, Great Books all over again — and this is precisely what has happened in many schools that now require a course in "literary theory." This, in my judgment, is a mistake. Even worse, it is just the kind of mistake that we English teachers can hardly help but make, and it leads to the kind of mistake that students can hardly help but make. We put a "theory" course in the curriculum. The students "take" the course. Been there, done that, on to the next course. We do this because we have been thoroughly indoctrinated in "coverage" as the organizational basis of our field. To change English from a field to a discipline, we shall have to change the way we think at a fundamental level. This can only be painful, especially at first.

A canon of methods, unlike a set of texts, must be conceived in terms of competence. There is no point in introducing students to the writing of Jacques Derrida, for example, if they finish their study unable to deconstruct a text and unaware of the strengths—and the limitations—of deconstruction as a way of reading and writing. A canon of methods must be organized in terms of the enhanced capabilities that students will take away from their studies. The end of such studies should be what I have called, in another context, textual power. Now, any attempt to organize a curriculum around students and their abilities is likely, at the present time, to run into criticism on the grounds that they are being taught skills instead of being given the knowledge that they need. This line of argument is familiar to most of us as an aspect of E. D. Hirsch's effort to promote a national curriculum in this country. There are, I believe, some strong arguments to be made for a national curriculum, though my curriculum would be different from Hirsch's. The opposition between skill and knowledge, however, is a red herring. And it leads to Hirsch's greatest error, the equation of coverage with knowledge. Knowledge that is not usable and regularly used is lost. The knowledge that we retain is the knowledge that we can and do employ. There is an important educational principle in the old saw about things that go in one ear and out the other. What we take in through our eyes and ears must emerge from our hands and mouths if we are to hold on to it. It is a curious property of information that we keep it only if we give it away. Material "covered" in classrooms and not incorporated into the communicative lives of students simply fades away.

A canon of methods, then, must be presented to students in the form of intellectual tools that they can use effectively. I outlined a set of basic courses in textual methods in Chapter 4, in the form of a new trivium, suitable for the general education of all students. Such a set of courses—or some other set that deals with the modes of thought and expression involved in those courses—would serve very well as the intellectual basis of English as a discipline.

With this kind of general education behind them, students specializing in English would already be well on their way toward mastering a canon of methods when they begin their more specialized work. If such a set of general education courses cannot be instituted—for whatever reasons—an English department could easily establish some version of them as part of its own core of study. This, at any rate, is one illustration of what I mean by putting theory and a canon of methods at the center of the discipline. Additional courses with more particular topics can easily be imagined as part of the full panoply of courses in methods offered within the discipline. The aim should be to open up possibilities, to empower. The graduates of English programs should have found the method or methods that work best for them as readers and writers—and they should know the virtues and the limitations of their preferred critical and interpretive methods. In practice, this means a reorientation of courses around the work of students, with a better balance between textual consumption and production. It is not what is covered that counts but what is learned. It is not what students have been told that matters but what they remember and what they can do. The New Critics understood this, as did their great opponent, Northrop Frye. Which brings me to another important point about literary theory and a canon of methods.

As I pointed out in Chapters 2 and 4, when our culture lost its faith in the historicism of Hegel—and that of Marx—we were left open to the domination of fashion. That is, if human history is not an ordained or determined progress toward truth and freedom, or toward a classless society, it can easily be seen as an essentially meaningless succession of cultural and political styles. If human existence is not a progressive dialectic organized by the Absolute (Hegel) or History (Marx), then it is all too easy to see it in terms of cultural relativism or even solipsism. In the great world of public affairs, this leads to the aggressive construction of false absolutes, whether religions or nations, along with the awareness that power settles all questions. The victors write history. The vanquished, if they are lucky, read it. In the little world of English departments, the failure of historicism leads, on the one hand, to teaching that is dangerously close to political indoctrination and, on the other, to "research" that is mainly an attempt to write about literary works in currently fashionable modes of analysis. Both of these problems are serious and complicated. They are also closely related. Let us try to trace their interrelation.

Modern culture—that culture in which we live and learn and teach—is characterized by the loss of faith in historicism and, along with that, a loss of faith in universal values of all sorts. In literary studies, this means that the idea of literature itself, as a kind of text found with common features in all human cultures, can no longer be taken for granted. Cleanth Brooks saw the problem fifty years ago and discussed it in a brilliant essay appended to *The Well-Wrought Urn* ("Criticism, History, and Critical Relativism," 215–51), in which he argued for a poetical quality that transcends the social and historical specificity of particular times and places. Northrop Frye, also, who was completely at odds with Brooks on the subject of whether taste is a part of literary criticism or a social epiphenomenon, nevertheless believed in a universal "order of words" and in the recurrence of archetypes and generic structures across languages and cultures. Their views, and others like them, are now dismissed out of hand by many teachers of English—especially among the younger generation of teachers. At the same time there are plenty of English teachers,

tion Army but rather kept until they can be renewed or replaced by something more truthful. To put this in simple and concrete terms, it means that theory, as our disciplinary core, must be careful about preserving its own past to avoid repeating it, whether as fashion or as farce. If, as I believe is the case, the New Critics said some important and durable things about poetry, we had better ensure that these things are not lost to our students and ourselves. And the same holds true for other advances in theory made by the Aristotelians of Chicago, the formalists of Petersburg, the structuralists of Prague, and so on. If we must be "post"-structuralist, it is up to us to make sure that we are dialectically—rather than merely fashionably—"post."

We need to recover, then, something of the historicist dialectic, even if we must play the directive role ourselves in the absence of the Absolute. But what about the replacement of the transcendental and literary in our classrooms by the political? This is a direct result of an awareness that not only history but literature as well is mainly written by the victors and the dominators or those who seek their favor, and this is true in the polite world of letters as well as in the larger world of political conquest. As one of Jane Austen's heroines so graciously says to a man who is denigrating the intelligence and achievements of women, "The pen has been in your hands." Indeed it has, and when pens came to be more generously distributed the podium was still closely guarded—which has made the scene of various struggles for representation shift from the places of publication to such places of interpretation as the classroom. Every English department in the United States is now in some phase of a struggle over how "minority" literatures in English—ethnic American, postcolonial, gay/lesbian—are to be represented in the curriculum and who, if anyone, is to teach them. One result of this struggle has been the development of courses in specialized literature taught by specialized faculty to specialized students. In such courses passions often run high. The Cuban-American community, to take just one example, is deeply divided on certain issues. But are they "literary" issues?

In a curriculum oriented to English literary history, such courses remain marginalized, and their proliferation is seen as a drain on the basic mission of covering the masterpieces of British and American literature. In a curriculum oriented to English textuality, however, such courses would have a vital function. What better place to apply and test modes of reading and writing than among texts that stir the passions? And what better way of refining those passions and guiding them into productive channels than the analytical discipline of textual theory? As a discipline, English needs both the cool rigor of theory and a passionate commitment to particular texts and ideas. Even as individual readers, we need them both. The political enters the study of English primarily through questions of representation: who is represented, who does the representing, who is object, who is subject—and how do these representations connect to the values of groups, communities, classes, tribes, sects, and nations? This happens, now, because in our culture people are aware that representation is an issue. This is not some aberration of the schools. It is the operation within them of the forces that permeate our whole culture. Eliminating the political is the fond hope of those nostalgic for the cultural homogeneity of Billy Phelps's classroom. But we cannot do it, now, and still be responsible educators. Responsibility here must take the form of establishing a disciplinary framework strong enough to allow the political full play in the study of textuality. By being responsible in this way, we will not suppress the power and beauty of language that have always been our concern. We will simply resituate them in a more rhetorical and less literary discipline of thought and study.

The political in the classroom, of course, sometimes takes the form of advocacy by teachers that can be offensive, if not repressive. This is by no means as widespread as certain critics of the academy have claimed that it is. On the other hand, it should not be surprising that ill-paid part-time teachers and graduate students facing dubious futures might hold political views different from those of the wealthy and powerful who sit on the governing bodies of colleges and universities. About this situation, which is real enough, I have two things to say. One, which I would address to those in power and those concerned about possible leftist indoctrination, is this: Don't worry. As the example of Althusser in Assignment 2 demonstrates so clearly, what students learn from teachers has more to do with how they teach than with what they teach. If indoctrination in schools really worked, Soviet-style communism would still prevail in Eastern Europe. But it doesn't. Which does not mean that bad teaching should be tolerated. Still, I would rather have my children educated by smart, caring people whose political values are different from mine than by dolts who agree with me politically. Finally, one must realize that the most oppressive indoctrination often results in the most powerful resistance.

The second thing I have to say on this question is addressed to those involved in the discipline of English. There is plenty of room for advocacy in this discipline, but no room at all for indoctrination. A discipline for which rhetoric is a central concern must be a discipline in which arguments on varying sides of important issues are admitted and considered—with one exception. If tolerance and a fair hearing for different views are at the core of the discipline, then arguments against tolerance and fairness are out of order and cannot be tolerated. Though I admit that one can never be absolutely impartial or perfectly just, I still believe, with C. S. Lewis, in the honest examiner who can give high marks to a strong argument, even while disagreeing with the conclusions. Now, more than ever, the graduates of our schools and colleges will live in worlds different from those in which they were born and went to school. A discipline called English must help them prepare for unknown conditions. The best preparation we can give our students will be the highest level of competence as readers and writers, producers and consumers of the various texts they will encounter. Tolerant, skeptical, interested in the truthfulness of a text and in the pleasure it may offer—this is the kind of gradu-

downright contradiction. How can we actually get more and better historical study into the curriculum while reconstructing the discipline around theory rather than literary history? The question is more than fair: it is crucial. My answer, though not simple, will be as clear as I can make it. First of all, to get serious about history means insisting that students concentrating in English take a responsible set of courses in the related historical disciplines: political history, intellectual history, art history, music history, history of science and technology, taught by faculty in those disciplines. This will undoubtedly mean a larger set of requirements for the major, though not more courses taught by the English department. This, in itself, would be a healthy counterstroke to the inclination of students to multiply the number of their majors, so that they finish with more credentials but with less learning and less usable knowledge. That is, they finish without a disciplined knowledge of any field of study. An English major with serious external requirements would make a genuine contribution to the reversal of the trend toward a "shopping mall curriculum"—a course of study without focus or concentration.

The idea is simple. Students should be free to choose their specializations. But that choice should represent a commitment to orienting their education around their chosen discipline. That is, instead of fulfilling in a halfhearted way an arbitrary set of "distribution requirements," students might satisfy the proper concern about the breadth of their education by a set of courses in various fields oriented to their major commitment—and given coherence by that orientation. We do so many things backward in education. We are always asking students to get certain requirements out of the way *before* they do something else. What I am suggesting is that the *need*—and, if possible, the desire—for certain kinds of knowledge be established in the minds of students before they begin to acquire it. In the present case, I would say, "Choose your area of interest and then get the broad educational background that will support your specialized study." As members of a discipline, an English faculty should be able to insist that students take a configuration of courses in other disciplines that will allow them to attain the competence and confidence that they seldom achieve at present. Obviously, this sort of thing will have to be negotiated with administrations and other faculties—but the results are bound to justify the trouble. And it is clear that what we are doing now is not good enough.

The second step in getting serious about the historical side of English as a discipline means rethinking the way history is approached within the English curriculum. And here I wish to propose, once again, reversing the way we have done things in the past. Thinking about the place of history within the English curriculum must begin by recognizing that history itself has not stopped during the two centuries in which English moved from the margins of humanistic education to near the center of it. In these centuries, developments in printing techniques, along with the invention of photography, film, and television, have resulted in a similar move by popular culture from the oral enclaves of the "folk" to the center of modern culture. It is this history, and the changes it has worked within the more traditional forms of textual production, that must organize the historical dimension of English studies. I am saying—insisting, if you like—that the old survey courses, which begin at the beginning and follow a narrow line of "masterpieces" until the end, no longer serve their purpose. It is not simply that the line is too narrow, though it is, but that this material does not reach students effectively because they do not know why they need it. I would go further. In many cases, it is not what they need most.

This is a complicated matter. I ask your patience while I try to address some of the complications. First of all, we must admit that there is no good argument against any kind of knowledge. Is it good to know *The Faerie Queene?* You bet it is—much better to know it than not to know it. It is better to know all six books, and the two Mutabilitie Cantos as well—not to mention Spenser's shorter poems, his role in the subjection of Ireland, his awareness of Italian models, and so on—than just to know Book One. But a curriculum is always a trade-off between knowledge and time. The question posed by every curriculum is "What knowledge is most crucial for students to have at this point in their education, and how much of that knowledge can they really acquire in the time and format available?" Both aspects of this question are important. That is, (1) what do students most need, and when are they readiest to learn it? and (2) how much of what they need can they be expected to learn in any given course or set of courses?

The historical knowledge that students of the discipline of English need the most is an understanding of the cultural changes that have taken place during the past two centuries, the centuries in which the modern media arose and came to dominate the cultures of the world. Such a knowledge, I am convinced, would enable students to discover that developments of great importance had preceded these two centuries, and would give them both motivation and direction in seeking out courses that would answer to their desire to understand the modern world more fully. Let me be as clear as I can be about this point. I think that the historical goal of English as a discipline should begin and end with where we—our students and ourselves— are now. What are the texts, the events, the ideas, and the forces that have made our present world and continue making it every day? How are we to understand this world—and which texts can tell us the most about it or currently have the most to do with shaping it? These are the questions that must be asked at the beginning of our historical inquiry and continue to be heard throughout that inquiry.

To put it simply, we must begin where we are, at the end, and start asking how we got here. In terms of a curriculum to sustain the historical dimension of the discipline of English, this means that most introductory courses should not be literary surveys that start at the "beginning" but rather courses in the culture of the modern period that accommodate the rise of the new media and situate traditional literary works among the texts of these upstart media. Beyond this I would like to see historical options for students in the form of courses that seek to connect earlier times and texts to our modern situation. At the level of ideas and values, what we think of as modern culture emerged from a struggle between Enlightenment notions of individual freedom and rationality, on the one hand, and challenges to those notions by the Romantic poets and by thinkers like Nietzsche and Freud, on the other. A course that explores this process, through a range of texts from the eighteenth to the twentieth century, can be very appealing to students who are committed to understanding modern culture and have some grounding in that culture from their introductory courses. I have personally taught such courses, including one that traced the rise and fall of aestheticism from the first uses of the term in the eighteenth century to modern portraits of artists in literature and other media, and I have found the subject matter, if well arranged, to be so powerfully engaging as to triumph over the most indifferent instruction.

The desire to learn is a fundamental human characteristic. Given half a chance, students take to historical learning avidly and gratefully. But our schools often manage to discourage such desires by courses that are poorly conceived, leading to knowledge that does not seem either interesting or useful. We can do better, and do so easily, if we will only drop a few preconceptions, like the need to cover everything and to start all historical studies at the earliest possible moment. We will also, of course, need to stop arranging syllabi of masterpieces like ducks in a row and start designing courses around topics and questions that connect the past to our present cultural situation.

Production

This is the part of English that is usually put beyond the pale (as "creative" writing) or down in the dungeon (as "composition"). Yet just the other day I sat in a room full of English professors and heard them complaining about the writing of their students. As I hope I made clear in Chapter 1, this is not a new complaint. What was most dispiriting about the conversation I attended, however, was that it seemed to presuppose writing to be a mere tool, something students ought to have picked up along the way. This is, to put it as mildly as my indignation will let me, not helpful. The ability to write well in a range of expressive modes ought to be a major and explicit goal of any discipline called English. This means that courses in which writing is a central concern should be given a serious place in the English curriculum—and that the writing of students should be given serious attention in every English course. In the standard English major, neither of these conditions prevails in the actual practice of teachers, whatever the departmental literature may claim to be the case. Most departments, however, would not even claim that they accept writing courses as the equal of reading courses in their curricula, because reading is actually called literature, while writing is just writing.

The way the invidious binary literature/composition plays out in English departments has been the object of my attention in an earlier book (*Textual Power,* chapter 1), so I will not go over that ground in any detail here. The key to solving the problem, however, is in the recognition that what the structuralists call literariness is a part of ordinary language and, in particular, is visible in most good writing. The condition I described in Chapter 1 of this book, in which students studied orations in order to become orators, cannot be repeated on the grand scale of contemporary education, no doubt, but it can still serve us as a useful model. Better reading and better writing go hand in hand. One of the uses of the best writers from the past (not the only one, but one) is that they provide models of syntactic and semantic possibilities. From Hooker, Donne, Swift, Johnson, Austen, Pater, Woolf, and Joyce we can learn something about life, to be sure, but we can also learn a lot about the possibilities of English prose. Students who are encouraged not only to read the major texts of the past but to pastiche and parody their styles will do a better job of getting inside the heads of those writers, and they will themselves become better writers because they have done so.

We are living, as some of our most acute thinkers keep reminding us, in an age of parody and pastiche. What is often called postmodernism is cultural production in which appropriation of the past plays a major part. Think of a production, now available on video, of Igor Stravinsky's modern opera *The Rake's Progress,* in which the narrative is derived from a sequence of engravings by the eighteenth-century English artist William Hogarth, presented in a production using a stunning visual setting designed by the contemporary painter David Hockney, with a libretto in which the modern poet W. H. Auden pastiches neoclassical writing even as Stravinsky pastiches the musical styles of Handel and Mozart. In an age like ours, pastiche and parody are the natural way into our cultural heritage. We should make better use of this route in making this heritage available to our students.

Production, in this age, must also mean film, video, and digital composition, for all of these use the verbal language as well as the languages of images and tones. An English department cannot do everything, of course, but literary study that cuts itself off from the performing and media arts risks going the way of classics. It was not a mistake for the rhetoric department at Berkeley to incorporate the study of film and television. To such departments the future will belong—or to English departments wise enough to embrace rhetoric and the media themselves and to find ways of connecting these contemporary texts to their more traditional concerns. In particular, writing for these media, and writing in hypertextual digital modes, should be seen by English departments as ways of maintaining their necessary connection to the culture around them—if they wish to play a major role in that culture.

That having been said, I want to add that "creative writing" faculties are now often a very conservative element in English departments. Think about it. You have faculties largely trained in modes of writing that are themselves becoming marginalized. Often, they espouse avant-gardist attitudes that are now ritualized gestures, paying tribute to a futurist or dadaist moment that is long gone. And they disdain what I have heard creative writing professors refer to as genre fiction—something they consider beneath their attention. No matter that some of the most exciting work in fiction now appears in the form of crime, espionage, and techno-fiction. So they go on offering courses in traditional modes of "creative" writing, including the now traditional avant-gardist sorts of experimental fiction. In this situation a genre like the essay, which has an excellent pedigree and is still flourishing, often falls through the cracks, being neither "creative" nor academic, though it is a useful mode for developing writers.

As I hope I have made plain, by giving production a larger place in the discipline of English, I do not just mean allowing credit for traditional courses in composition or creative writing within the English major. I am asking for a rethinking of what writing and other modes of linguistic production have to offer students, and a reconstruction of the courses themselves. Those who teach students how to write poetry, fiction, and drama have never expected all their students, or even most of them, to become professional writers of stories, poems, and plays. They have always believed, however—and many have said this to me—that their students would be better readers of literature because of their attempts to write it. And they are right, I have no doubt. What is necessary, now, is for the discipline as a whole to accept this position and to rethink the role of writing in English studies with few preconceptions beyond the goal of producing the most literate students possible. This will mean, as I have been arguing, both new kinds of courses and a new relation between reading and writing in the courses being taught.

Consumption

It is no accident that what English departments consider their principal reason for being comes last in this list of four functions, and under a heading that suggests either the old name for a dreaded disease or the driving force behind a market economy. This ungracious heading also displaces attention from the quasi-sacred textual object,

Literature, to the process by which such objects are assimilated or ingested: consumption. All this is deliberate, tendentious, and possibly unfair. It is also necessary, for the notion of literature as something to be professed, something that carries its own transcendental justification, is deeply embedded in the thinking of English teachers, to the point where it seriously inhibits reconstructing the discipline. Throughout this book I have been giving reasons why I believe this way of thinking about texts is no longer useful, but it is so deeply ingrained that I fear even one more attempt to dislodge it may not be sufficient. Let me try once again. I will attempt to make my point in a manner sufficiently different from my earlier efforts to afford some mild amusement for those who have already taken it.

What sacred texts offer within their own cultures can be described as the Truth, or the Way. They tell believers how things are—and how to live. Secular texts cannot offer the same consolations with the same absolute conviction. To read the Bible as literature is to secularize it. To read *Middlemarch* (to name a work with serious ethical aspirations, written by a woman who knew her Bible, as well as many other things) is to read a text that aspires to a certain kind of authority: the right to generalize about human nature, to say "we" and make it stick. This is not a despicable power, but, since the author is neither God nor inspired by a divinity, we are not obliged to believe what the author tells us nor to act as she advises us. If we do believe, and if we do try to act as she suggests we should, it is because of the power of the examples and arguments she puts before us. No despicable power, as I said, but a rhetorical power, not a fundamental power. The intellectual situation that I am attempting to describe is an ancient one, the divine in opposition to the secular, the absolute opposed to the relative, the True text as opposed to the Rhetorical one.

For our purposes, what is most interesting about this opposition is the place of the literary text in relation to the sacred and the secular. Plato, in a certain mood, was quite ready to push poetry over to the rhetorical side and exile it from his ideal state. Aristotle, who held his nose in order to produce a handbook of rhetoric, nevertheless found a secular use for poetic drama—it purged pity and fear from the minds of citizens, thus enabling them to use those minds for thinking about civic matters. Romantic aestheticians and their followers have tried to push poetry or literature back toward the sacred, as partaking of the oversoul, the primary imagination, or universal archetypes. From this we should learn that literature, sometimes called poetry, has no fixed place but changes its position and function as cultures change. English departments rode Pegasus to a position of academic prestige and relative affluence, but now, in our time, Pegasus has begun to look like other extremely large creatures with wings, that run very fast but can't get off the ground. The myths tell us that such creatures put their heads in the sand to avoid unpleasant or threatening sights. But what do myths know?

In the age of mass media, literature has, as Walter Benjamin put it, lost its aura. We can either pretend, ostrichwise, that this has not happened, or decide what to do about it. As you might expect, I am all for doing something about it. Indeed, I welcome the opportunity. This is the chance, this is the moment, to change reading from a passive to an active process. This is the moment to replace priestly exegesis and passive coverage with attention to reading as a process. The idea is not new. In 1818 the young John Keats, in a letter to his friend Reynolds, urged reading only a few things, perhaps a single page, and letting that lead to "a voyage of conception." Keats called this process a "delicious, diligent Indolence," and went on to describe it in a lovely metaphor:

> Now it appears that almost any Man may like the spi-
> der spin from his own inwards his own airy Citadel
> —the points of leaves and twigs on which the spi-
> der begins her work are few, and she fills the air with
> a beautiful circuiting. Man should be content with
> as few points to tip with the fine Web of his Soul,

> and weave a tapestry empyrean full of symbols for
> his spiritual eye, of softness for his spiritual touch, of
> space for his wandering, of distinctness for his luxury.
> (Keats, 79)

Keats, through his Romantic vocabulary of soul and spirit, is talking about reading as a creative process, and his metaphor is the metaphor of textuality, the spider weaving her web, creating something new, which is strung from a few leaves and twigs already in place but is nevertheless unique and beautiful. The human reader, like the spider, should create a "tapestry" that depends upon a few previous texts but is the reader's own creation, offering solace and stimulus. The play of Keats's own mind, as he reaches for difficult concepts here, leads him to weave a web of paradox and oxymoron—especially in the root concept of "diligent Indolence," which animates the whole passage. The New Critics would be quick to tell us that this is a sign of the presence of poetry itself, and the structuralists would call it literariness. And they would be right.

Such concepts, and others like them, ought to be a part of the reading equipment of all readers, and especially of those readers who are trained in the discipline of English. I am suggesting that Keats offers us more than one thing from which we can learn in this passage. The simple message that a few texts well-pondered may be more valuable than many texts consumed thoughtlessly—that is just one of the things we can learn from the passage. Another is the rhetorical power of images, like that of the spider. Others are the poetical power of the paradox, and the rhetorical power of oxymoron. To read this passage fully, of course, would be to look for the intertextual twigs and leaves from which it hangs, to see where this vocabulary of soul weaving comes from, to explore the other letters and the life of Keats, to see, for instance, how he was, in fact, reading quite a lot in those days, especially Shakespeare, and constantly dropping allusions into his letters. To read the letters of Keats is to wish to know him better. And to know him better, it is clear, one must know Shakespeare as well.

What am I trying to say about the consumption of texts, otherwise known as reading? Let me try to boil my thoughts down to a few twigs and leaves, or, as Ezra Pound would put it, an abc of reading:

a. The process of reading should take precedence over the coverage of texts in the English curriculum. By process I mean learning how to read closely and carefully, how to situate a text in relation to other texts (intertextuality), how to situate a text in relation to culture, society, the world (extratextuality). Let me give some very simple examples of this. I recently saw two bumper stickers. Admittedly, bumper stickers are a very modest form of textuality, but reading them requires, in little, many of the skills required for texts of greater consequence. One of these bumper stickers, on an old VW Beetle, read this way: "God is coming, and Is She Pissed!" Inelegant? Yes. Vulgar, even blasphemous? Certainly. But, like much blasphemy, theologically interesting. In reading this text five moves are crucial. One is the intertextual move, in which the reader connects this text to many others that announce the end of the world or the Second Coming. This begins as another such eschatological statement. The second move is also intertextual but at a less specific level. The feminine pronoun, "She," comes as a shock because of all those other Judeo-Christian texts in which "He" is used, and all those visual texts that represent God as distinctly male. The third move is to note the shift of register in the last word, which makes the whole second clause idiomatic, vulgar, and arresting. "Pissed" is short for "pissed off," which is colloquial for angry. Which brings us to the fourth move, the move to interpretation, in which we consider the significance of what we have already noted and seek the meaning (or most prominent meanings) of this little text. The vulgarity is mainly an attention getter, meant to shock us. It works because the notion of an angry God has been very pervasive in Jewish and Christian thought (think of Jonathan Edwards's representation of him, for instance). Reducing the divine wrath to the level of urine is funny because of the incongruity. Is there a contrast between this liquid and the fires of hell—or is that going too far with interpretation?—questions to be debated. Finally, the text invites us to assume that thousands of years of being represented by the wrong gender might indeed be a justification for a bit of pique. The fifth move, extratextual but still a part of reading, is to consider the place of the text in the world—in this case an ancient Beetle, a sixties car, a feminist text, which leads to guesses about the owner—possibly wrong ones—and to the reasons for this particular display. Learning to read is all about the ability to make intellectual moves like these—and to make them on texts more complicated and difficult than this one.

The second bumper sticker is one I first noticed on a battered pickup truck: "If you don't like my driving, call 1-800-EAT-SHIT." Reading this one is easy in one sense, but a good reading of it requires both information and speculative thought. The information required is intertextual. We need to know a few different things. One is that business telephone numbers often use the formula 1-800, followed by seven letters that spell memorable words, often following the traditional grouping of telephone numbers, so that a three-digit exchange followed by a four-digit individual number turns into a three-letter word followed by a four-letter word. This is possible only because our phones group letters with every number on their buttons save zero and one. In this case, of course, the four-letter word is a four letter word, an obscenity of sorts, rather similar in that respect to the last word of the other bumper sticker. Making the last word a shocker begins to look like a part of the poetic diction of the genre, though our sample is too small to support any generalizations. One is not advised to dial the number, in any case. So far in our reading, the text appears to be a mere insult. I think it is an insult, but not so mere as it first appears to be. If we do a little intertextual digging, we should recall a related formula that appears on the back of larger trucks, inviting people to call an actual number if the driver is not competent or courteous. Presumably, this invitation to get the driver in trouble is not put there by the driver but by his or her employers. It is a kind of advertising, seeking goodwill, and a kind of threat for the driver as well.

Intertextual knowledge of the standard invitation to report bad driving is required for a strong, rich reading of the sign on the pickup truck. To round off the reading, we need only imagine that the driver who owns the pickup truck either also drives a larger vehicle for hire, which displays the invitation to snitch, or simply wants to register solidarity with other truck drivers and assert his or her own independence. Even this very simple and clearly vulgar text, then, invites a skilled, imaginative reading rather than a perfunctory dismissal as beneath both contempt and interpretation. The process of reading involved in both these tiny texts is the same as that required on a grander scale for more ambitious works. And it should be discussed explicitly in classes and demonstrated frequently by students, over a range of textual modes from different times and places.

b. The reading of modern and recent texts can play a major part in whetting the appetite of students for earlier literature. I can imagine a course in which a reading of Keats, starting with his letters, leads to a reading of some of Shakespeare's plays, as Keats was reading them. Keats, of course, was going to the theater, seeing Shakespeare in performance, writing about actors, attending lectures, writing about lecturers. To understand him rightly means understanding his cultural situation, his social situation, the places he lived in, his world. I can also imagine a course in which a reading of Scott Fitzgerald leads to a reading of Keats, for Fitzgerald loved Keats and, in his own letters, urged his daughter to read the poet. One could go on and on.

c. Students should learn to read a range of texts, from various times and places, in various genres and media, in "high" and "low" forms of textuality. If English teachers have done a good job of teaching reading in the past, they have done it mostly by teaching a reverent approach to masterpieces. Such an approach has its uses, but it is not good training for reading the highly manipulative texts of advertising and propaganda and other persuasive forms. It is not even a complete training in reading literature, because even masterpieces often have a large component of propaganda and manipulation. Good reading involves reading every text sympathetically, trying to get inside it, to understand the intentionality behind its composition. It also involves reading every text unsympathetically, critically—but the sympathetic has to come first or the critical reading is impossible. If we impose our own values on every text, we have nothing to criticize but ourselves. Reading, as I have argued in several other books, involves an attribution of intention, a sympathetic attempt to discern that intention, and a critical distancing and examination of that intention. One might, for instance, utterly reject the sentiments offered in the two bumper stickers discussed above, but the only informed basis for such a rejection depends upon a prior sympathetic reading.

Reading advertisements, reading films and television shows, reading political speeches, reading poems, plays, essays, stories, and everything else under the sun—this is what we should be teaching. If one were to attempt to "cover" all this, of course, the task would be impossible. No set of teachers or students can possibly do it all. The present curriculum based on coverage, however, is also impossible—we just pretend it isn't by lining up some masterpieces chronologically and calling that literary history. What we need is a greater variety of courses, with a constant and prevailing emphasis on the process of reading, along with whatever constraints on choices that a given faculty thinks appropriate for the best results. Should students know some of the major writers from the early periods of English and American literature? Of course, and departments should set their requirements to make sure this happens. But they should also arrange courses so that all students develop their reading skills as early as possible and continue deepening and enriching them as they progress through the curriculum. That students who graduate in English

should be excellent readers, ready to encounter unfamiliar texts, to
situate them, interpret them, and criticize them—these are the goals
of an English education with respect to the consumption of texts.

PRACTICAL PROBLEMS—AND SOLUTIONS

What I have just described as a discipline of English oriented around
the theory, history, production, and consumption of texts will be difficult to achieve because it requires a massive shift in priorities as well
as many practical changes in courses and curricula, but it is far from
impossible, because people are doing many of these things already,
though they may not be consciously perceiving them as stages in a
total reorientation of English from a field of study to a discipline.
At the present time, however, English departments, especially those
in large universities, face an array of practical problems that often
seem more urgent than the kind of theoretical reorientation I have
been urging. Many of these problems have causes that lie outside the
academy, in the national culture or economy, for instance, but they
are nonetheless problems that English departments and university
administrators must solve at their own level. At this point, with some
diffidence, I will try to describe the most pressing of these practical
problems and suggest some solutions. Without wishing to argue that
the sort of intellectual reconstruction of the discipline that I have
been proposing will solve any of these practical problems, I do indeed want to claim that such a reorientation will make it easier to
recognize them, to face them, and to make the necessary changes in
policy. Some of the problems overlap one another. I will try to take
them one at a time and shift focus when the overlap becomes acute.

The first problem I wish to examine is that of graduate study
in English, which, as we shall see, overlaps with the problem of the
nature of research in the field. The Ph.D. in English, as presently
constituted, is a research degree, designed to train graduate students
to produce "original research" (which means research worthy of pub-

lication) in some part of the field of English. It functions, however, as the necessary qualification for most teaching positions in four-year colleges and universities. The *research* degree as the primary credential for a *teaching* position is such an established part of higher education that we can scarcely see the oddity of it. I should say at once that I see no problem in requiring mastery of a field or discipline in order to teach it, nor am I a great believer in degrees in "teaching" without such mastery of an academic subject. The problem is not with learning in itself but with research as the only acceptable way of demonstrating mastery—and in particular, with publication as the only acceptable way of demonstrating that research has indeed been done. This is the Germanic model of graduate study, introduced into the United States in the later nineteenth century; moreover, it is this model as influenced by the scientific and quantitative disciplines. In the humanities, this model is no longer working very well. That is part of the problem with graduate studies at the moment, but it is by no means the whole of it.

The other major part of the problem—and especially the problem with the Ph.D. degree—is that every year English departments produce about twice as many graduates with this degree as would be required to fill all the positions that are open in the field. Every year, then, more candidates remain unemployed or in temporary jobs, waiting to compete against the new graduates the following year. This results in a high degree of competitiveness for those scarce positions, which takes the form of demanding more and more in the way of "research" from candidates for positions with their newly minted or recent Ph.D. degrees in hand. The effects of this situation run broad and deep throughout the profession. Morale in graduate programs is disastrous. Students are reluctant to finish their degrees. As a result, they begin to form or join labor unions to protect what seems to be not a transient phase of their educational progress but a permanent way of academic life. Exploitation runs rampant in this situation, making unionization an appropriate response. There are two separate but related problems here. One is with the economic power of the degree in a depressed job market. The other is with the intellectual value of the degree as preparation for actually doing those scarce jobs once they are obtained.

Are graduate students in English learning what they most need to know and getting the experience they really need? Too often, the answer to these questions is that they are not. The pressures of the job market are changing the shape of graduate study for the worse, leading to the production of instant "research" by people who are simply unready to produce it, being thin in their general background and shallow even in their special fields—something I felt personally back in 1959 (see Assignment 1) but now see as more acute and more pervasive. This situation is an aspect of what I discussed in Chapter 2 as a loss of truthfulness in academic study—a turning away from any commitment to truth as the proper end of academic study. The idea of academic research as a "contribution to knowledge," the idea of "original research," requires an assumption of progress toward more adequate descriptions of reality. In the sciences, research receives its justification and its support—despite all the lip service to "pure" knowledge—from the exploitable discoveries or patents to which it may lead. In the humanities, research receives its justification—despite all the lip service to the advancement of learning—from its applicability to teaching. In fact, I would say that all important research in the humanities is simply teaching by other means than the lecture or the seminar. And conversely, published work in English studies that has no use in teaching or makes no contribution to learning is unimportant—trifling stuff. When Chaucer said of his Oxford Clerk that he would gladly learn and gladly teach, he was implying that the two activities were connected by more than the repeated adverb. Learning and teaching justify one another and support one another. But the pressure for research in English is often in direct conflict with both learning and teaching. And that is a formula for academic disaster—a disaster that is most obvious and most pressing in the situation of graduate studies in English.

The demand for research—and this is widely known—has led to a vast production of articles and books that are published and disappear without a trace. No one even pretends any longer to "keep up" with everything published on even a single major author. There is an eerie hollowness about the enterprise that is one sign of hypocriticism at work. There are indeed some interesting and useful books and articles published every year, and even some of the least significant work shows signs of academic ability and intelligence. But there is a vast effort here, an enormous expenditure of time and energy, that might have been much better spent on matters that bear more directly on the classroom. This situation, as I have said, is widely understood—yet, as with the weather, no one does anything about it. Why is this the case? It is partly because it is not easy to change a system so vast, with so much inertia behind it, but it is also because the testing of ideas in a public exchange with one's peers is a healthy developmental activity. What is wrong with this system is not that it requires intellectual exchange but that intellectual exchange has to masquerade as part of a progress toward the truth—in an academic culture that has largely forgotten truthfulness or consciously rejected it as a possibility.

There are two possible solutions to this dilemma. One is to say that, since truth is out of the question, what we have here is just conversation, with the prizes going to the best conversationalists. This is more or less the Fish/Rorty solution (though there are signs that Fish is changing his position, which I shall discuss before concluding). It has the virtue of ending hypocriticism at the expense of installing cynicism at the heart of the enterprise. Personally, I do not feel this to be much of an improvement. The other alternative is to find a way to reinstate the search for truth, now "disciplined," as Hegel said of Christianity, by the exposure to relativism and cynicism. Personally,

I believe that we sometimes arrive at the truth, that some questions are settled and need not be asked anymore. The earth is not a perfect sphere, but we know it is not flat. Still, even if we never complete our journey toward truth, it is important that we travel in the name of truthfulness, for, without this, the journey loses interest, for ourselves and for those we ask to share it with us. What makes Nietzsche interesting to us is the possibility that he may be right about important matters—even if we wish he were wrong. Even more important, his work is interesting because he wants to be right and wants to show that others have been wrong—which means that he needs to know very well what those others have said and meant. What would Derrida be without his struggles with Husserl, with Hegel? Operating under the sign of truthfulness, the desire to get things right, academic discourse can be valuable, even exciting. But this kind of truthfulness requires learning, which is to the humanities what experiment is to the sciences. When academic discourse turns away from truthfulness and embraces fashion, it requires a forgetting or ignorance of its own past, in order to achieve a spurious originality. Such work, even for the forgetful reader, lacks the energy and intensity that comes only from playing with the high stakes of truth and falsehood, getting it right and getting it wrong.

In my discussion of Althusser as a student in Assignment 2, I suggested that it may not be our "truth" that students learn from us, but the way of seeking truth that constitutes our integrity as scholars, the discursive habits by which we reach our conclusions and report on them. This view of a professional ideal may seem distant from the practical problems of developing future teachers in graduate school—but it is not. If we keep in mind the goal of preparing young scholars not just to follow methodological fashions but to master a discipline well enough to teach it and to share their ideas with peers in a common search for truth, we can use this goal to interrogate our present practices and consider alternatives, as I shall attempt to do in the following paragraphs.

The problem of graduate studies in English does not easily admit of unilateral solutions. Any single program that gets out of step with the others risks encountering either even worse results in placing its graduates or losses in prestige (within its own academic base as well as outside) that it would prefer not to endure, because the effects would entail economic as well as other consequences within the present system of academic rewards and punishments. Yet I would like to offer a few suggestions that the boldest and best programs might essay, which, if they work well, should encourage others to follow. I think things are bad enough for the Faustian phrase I used in Chapter 2 to apply here. We should not go on living like this. At any rate, as one excessively manacled and pinioned prisoner says to the other in a popular cartoon, "Here's my plan":

No half-measures—a comprehensive rethinking of the Ph.D. program or nothing. To put matters with brutal simplicity, I believe that a strong department could easily admit fewer students, keep them longer, treat them better, and prepare them much more successfully to compete in what is clearly going to remain a very difficult job market. At present, most Ph.D. students are in their programs for a nominal five years, which in practice gets to be six, seven, or even more. Suppose, instead of that, a program that admittedly lasted ten years, but with several of those years consisting of full-time teaching, with a course load comparable to what these teachers would be likely to have in their first full-time jobs. Suppose further that between the years of full-time teaching they would be awarded years of full-time study, fully supported. Planning to support them for ten years instead of five, departments would admit only half as many graduate students as they now do. Such a program could be economically viable for both the schools and the individuals, because graduate students currently carry a teaching load of roughly one-third as many courses as they will teach when working full-time. Sketched crudely, the plan would be something like this: a first year of courses and study, a second year of part-time, supervised teaching and some study, a third year of part-time teaching and study, a fourth year of study, a fifth year of full-time teaching, a sixth year of study, after which instructor status would be awarded, and then four alternate years of instruction and study, with the degree awarded at the end of this time or earlier if all requirements were satisfied. The result would be fewer graduates, who would finish their studies with real teaching experience, and, if their programs were properly designed, real learning as well.

Within such a program there would be much room for variations, but I would myself suggest that the number of official graduate courses and seminars now offered by most programs could be sharply reduced, allowing those senior faculty to teach more undergraduates, and that graduate students should do most of their work as directed study or independent research, in connection with whatever structure of examinations and productive work the faculty might devise. As I indicated above, the years of full-time teaching would make the years of supported study economically feasible for many schools. I have said nothing about dissertations or other forms of research and publication, but I think the kind of structural change I have suggested would accommodate itself to traditional forms of productive study as well as to innovations. I also believe, most firmly, that the alternation of full-time teaching and full-time study would allow teaching and learning to support one another in the happiest and most productive manner. And the ten-year program looks long only when compared to the nominal five-year programs that no longer operate as they are supposed to but often run on and on. Ten years with sufficient support to avoid going deeply into debt, as many graduate students do these days, would also be much better than seven or eight years with a serious debt problem and a degree that is no more than a hunting license for jobs that seem to belong to an endangered species.

Such programs, I am suggesting, would produce extremely attractive graduates, so that the forces of the market itself might lead to emulation, which in turn would result in a serious reduction in the total number of graduates produced each year, giving all such graduates a better chance for a decent academic life. And with senior faculty teaching more undergraduate course, we might begin to find ways to make teaching itself more consequential in the evaluation of faculty, programs, and entire schools. This is a change that seems to be coming these days, but it is being delayed by perceived problems in the evaluation of teaching. Such a qualitative art has not lent itself easily to quantitative evaluation. I believe, however, that truly concerned departments and administrations can find ways of getting better information about how their faculties are doing as teachers, and ways of rewarding faculty on the basis of that information. There are many sources of such information not even being considered now. If an English department, for instance, asked all its graduating seniors to list the three members of that faculty in whose courses they had learned the most, that department would, in several years, have an extremely useful body of information, much more useful than the little surveys taken on the spot at the end of particular courses. I would also suggest—and here administrations will need to play a leading role—that the quality of learning and thinking in lectures, articles, and books be given more weight in evaluations than the quantity. It is, of course, easier to count or measure than to read and evaluate, but this change can be made if the will to make it is present. Too much reliance is now put on perfunctory outside reviews, where internal evaluation might serve better. And far too much stress is placed upon quantity of publication than on the quality of learning and teaching displayed in writing, lectures, course designs, and assignments for student work.

A lot of what I have been talking about is a matter of changes in procedure that might be effected whether or not one reconceives of English as a discipline. And I would hope that some of these suggestions might make sense even to those who reject my larger argument. But these changes have come to my mind as aspects of reconstructing English as a discipline around a core of methods that are essentially pedagogical. That is, once we think of English in terms of what this study will enable students to do with texts, and think of what a teacher needs to learn so that he or she will have something to offer students of textuality, it becomes natural to rethink the production of teachers along the same lines—and by "production of teachers" I mean both what teachers produce and how they are themselves produced. With a shared disciplinary core of knowledge about textuality, we should be able to tolerate a wider range of particular interests among our faculty and offer a more interesting range of courses to our students, always remembering that our justification as teachers lies in what our students accomplish after they leave us. We need to give them the best and most flexible tools for a future that will be more theirs than ours.

One final problem should not be avoided here, and that is the balance of subfields within any given English department. At present, the actual history of English departments, supported by the shaping of the field around the literary history of England and America, has left many such departments with too many faculty in the earlier periods of English literature and not enough in American literature and the emerging subfields of Anglophone literatures, both postcolonial and ethnic American—and with far too many of the courses students actually want being taught by graduate students and part-time faculty. In a sense, to recognize this distribution of fields as a problem is to solve it, but such recognition is resisted by entrenched faculties. As I write, major universities are reporting large decreases in the number of English majors. Tinkering with the old curriculum will not solve these problems. What is needed is a paradigm shift from thinking of English as a field to thinking of it as a discipline. Thomas Kuhn warned us that paradigms are changed not by persuasion of those who hold the old ones but by their dying off and being replaced by people who have embraced the new. What will happen to English studies and the old paradigm of literary history remains to be seen, but the choice seems clear: adapt or dwindle, ending, perhaps, with a whimper.

Closing Down, Opening Up

The discipline of English is not a topic on which one should even aspire to say the last word. I have been trying to give a certain focus to a discussion that is already going on about the function of English in American education. Perhaps I can sharpen that focus by comparing my position to that taken by Stanley Fish in his recent book *Professional Correctness*. In this book Fish joins hands with John Crowe Ransom, declaring his agreement "with Ransom's insistence that it is a requirement for the respectability of an enterprise that it be, or at least be able to present itself as, *distinctive*" (Fish, 17, emphasis in original). The enterprise in question, for Ransom, was the one that English departments were (or should be) undertaking. For Fish, the enterprise can be called, quite simply, literary criticism, which he sees as the disciplinary core of English studies. He is insistent that literary criticism or interpretation must be at the center of English studies, because it is the one distinctive thing that such departments have to offer the world. His book, as a whole, is an argument against attempts to politicize the field of English instruction or to move such studies away, in any direction, from the central activity of asking "What is this poem (or novel or drama) saying?" (Fish, 25).

Fish is as insistent as I have been (and as Ransom and Frye were before us) that English studies ought to be a discipline. But in his zeal to protect literary studies from political excesses and false pretensions to cultural influence, he feels obliged to circle the wagons around a very narrow definition of literature that corresponds to a very specialized mode of reading. He also completely ignores the teaching of writing as a potential disciplinary core. In short, he seeks to ratify the domination of rhetoric by literature. What I have been proposing, on the other hand, is a discipline based on rhetoric and the teaching of reading and writing over a broad range of texts. Agreeing with Fish, and with Ransom and Frye, about the need for English to maintain a distinctive disciplinary core, I disagree with him—and the others, as well—in believing that the concept of textuality, which includes literariness but is not limited to it, can best serve that function. I welcome his book, however, as a sign that a professional figure of some consequence, on an important occasion (the Clarendon Lectures, delivered at Oxford in 1993), has shared my concern about the state of the profession and proposed a solution that, however different, should help to open the way to further discussion about the possibilities of English as a discipline. Let the discussion continue.

Yale Curriculum of 1822–23

Shortly after the establishment of the Professorship of Rhetoric and Oratory at Yale, the following curriculum was required of all students in the college. At that time, each of the four years was divided into three terms, with the third term a bit shorter than the others.

Freshman Class
  First term
    Livy begun
    Adams' Roman Antiquities
    Webber's Arithmetic revised
    Murray's English Grammar
  Second term
    Livy continued through five books
    Elegantiae Latinae
    Graeca Majora, the Historical parts
    Day's algebra
  Third term
    Morse's Geography
    Murray's Grammar reviewed
Sophomore Class
  First term
    Graeca Majora continued
    Playfair's Euclid begun
    Horace begun

Second term
> Day's Mathematics, Parts II and III
> Graeca Majora continued
> Cicero de Officiis begun

Third term
> Day's Mathematics, Part IV
> Conic Sections and Spheric Geometry
> Jamieson's Rhetoric
> Cicero de Officiis, de Senectute, and de Amicitia, finished

Junior Class
> First term
>> Spheric Trigonometry
>> Graeca Majora, finished
>> Enfield's Philosophy begun
>> Cicero de Oratore begun

> Second term
>> Homer's Iliad
>> Enfield's Philosophy continued
>> Cicero de Oratore continued
>> Tacitus, omitting the Annals

> Third term
>> Enfield's Astronomy
>> Tytler's History
>> Fluxions, Greek or Hebrew (at the option of the student)

Senior Class
> First term
>> Blair's Rhetoric
>> Hedge's Logic
>> Locke's Essays

> Second term
>> Paley's Natural Theology
>> Stewart's Philosophy of the Mind

Third term
   Paley's Moral Philosophy
   Paley's Evidences of Christianity

This curriculum is quoted directly from the Yale catalogue for 1822–23 (reprinted photographically in Pierson, 1983, 214–15). On the next page of the catalogue are listed a number of other required lectures and recitations. Among them are the following: "The members of the several classes attend also the private exercises and lectures of the Professor of Rhetoric and Oratory. Specimens of English Composition are exhibited daily by one or more of each of the divisions of the Sophomore and Junior classes. Written translations from Latin authors are presented by the Freshman class. The lower classes are also instructed in Latin Composition. The Senior and Junior classes have Forensic Disputations once or twice a week, before their instructors. There are very frequent exercises in Declamation, before the Tutors, before the Professor of Oratory, and before the Faculty and students in the chapel."

From this evidence we can get a fairly clear picture of the early development of "English" at Yale College. Such literature as there was in this curriculum appeared in the ancient languages, and even this was scanty. In Greek, students worked from an anthology for two years (beginning with the "historical parts") and then studied the *Iliad* in their third year. In Latin they read Livy's historical narratives, a bit of Horace, and then settled down for serious work in Cicero, reading three works of moral philosophy before concentrating for two terms in their junior year on his major work on rhetoric, *De Oratore,* along with the highly rhetorical prose of the Roman historian Tacitus. This was a curriculum in which little literature (as we understand the term) appeared, though Locke's philosophical essays were read in the senior year. The grammar of English got serious attention during the freshman year (one term of study and one of review), while logic and rhetoric were studied formally in the last year. Throughout the years, of course, students were producing compositions and giving oral disputations and declamations. The English language, rhetoric, and logic were a serious part of the curriculum, and they were reinforced by the materials and practices of the classical curriculum, by means of written translations, compositions in Latin, and study of rhetorically oriented works in the ancient languages.

This was the picture of college studies at Yale in 1822. The situation at the other small colleges functioning in this country at that time was similar.

The Course of Study Prescribed by the Laws of Rhode Island College in 1783

The President and Tutors, according to their judments, shall teach and instruct the several Classes in the learned Languages and in the liberal Arts and Sciences, together with the vernacular Tongus— The following are the classics appointed for the first year, in Latin, Virgil, Cicero's Orations and Horace, all in usum Delphini. In Greek, the new Testament, Lucians Dialogues and Zenophon's Cyropaedia;—For the second year, in Latin, Cicero de Oratore & Caesars Commentaries;—in Greek Homer's Iliad & Longinus on the sublime, together with Lowth's vernacular Grammar [of English], Rhetoric, Wards Oratory, Sheridan's Lectures on Elocution, Guthrie's Geography, Kaims Elements of Criticism, Watts's and Duncan's Logic.—For the third year, Hutchinson's moral Philosophy, Dodridges Lectures, Fennings Arithmatic, Hammonds Algebra, Stones Euclid, Martins Trigonometry, Loves Surveying, Wilsons Navigation, Martins Philosophia Britannica, & Ferguson's Astronomy, With Martin on the Globes.—In the last year, Locke on the Understanding, Kennedy's Chronology and Bollingbroke on History; and the Languages, Arts & Sciences, studied in the foregoing years, to be accurately reviewed. (Bronson, 103, all spellings as given)

Chronicle of the Demise of Rhetoric at Brown

In 1830, when Tristram Burges stopped giving instruction in oratory and belles lettres, his duties were taken over for a time by the professor of moral philosophy. In 1840 these duties were divided and the work given to two men, one teaching belles lettres and the other rhetoric. This marks the beginning of the long process by which English emerged from the division of eloquence into oratory and literature. In 1851 the Rev. Robinson P. Dunn appears in the catalogue as Professor of Rhetoric and English Literature. Though the professor's duties combined the two fields, this is the first time that English literature was named as such in the catalogue of Brown University.

In 1868, Timothy Whiting Bancroft assumed Dunn's professorship. In 1882 he was joined by an instructor in elocution. In 1886 a second instructor in rhetoric and modern languages was added. In 1889 the Brown catalogue began to list Departments of Instruction (as opposed to a partial list of Departments of Practical Science). In this new list the Department of Rhetoric and English Literature is so named for the first time. In 1890 the whole faculty in this department consisted of Bancroft, Lorenzo Sears as an associate professor of rhetoric, and an instructor in elocution. But rapid changes were on the way. One year later the departmental list included a Department of Rhetoric and Oratory followed by a separate Department of English Literature and Language. The faculty consisted of an associate professor of rhetoric and an instructor in elocution, on the one hand, and a professor of English language and literature with an instructor in English, on the other. In the next few years these departments grew, mainly through an increase in instructors and a still lower rank called assistants, but rhetoric grew the most. In 1894, Brown had one faculty member in English language, one in literature, and five in rhetoric and elocution, with six assistants in rhetoric. This was the high-water mark of rhetoric at Brown. (All data about Brown without a specific citation have come directly from the Brown catalogues for these years in the John Hay Library.)

In 1895 one of the rhetoric faculty, Lorenzo Sears, changed his title to associate professor of American literature. He was the first to hold a title that included American literature at Brown, and the only one for a long while. In 1896 there were four faculty in English and two in rhetoric, plus four assistants, who worked in the basic course, Practical Rhetoric. At this time there were no courses in rhetoric or composition in the English department, but Practical Rhetoric, in the rhetoric department, was becoming more like our modern composition courses. In the English department the first course, English 1, 2, 3, was now a prerequisite for advanced work in English. This course consisted of "greater poets and prose writers from Spenser to Arnold." In 1897–98 the order of the departments list changed, with the Department of English Literature and Language preceding the Department of Rhetoric for the first time. Among the offerings in English literature were English 4, 5, 6; Shakspeare (spelled this way in many college catalogues until the twentieth century); and individual courses in Spenser, Bacon, and Milton; plus period courses in Dryden to Cowper, Burns to Keats, the Victorians, the nineteenth-century essay, and American literature.

In 1900 the rhetoric department was eliminated, swallowed up by the Department of English Literature and Language. It went from its zenith to oblivion in six short years. Practical Rhetoric became English 1, 2, 3 and was required of all freshmen. Most of the old rhetoric curriculum appeared as the five lowest courses in English, but even the last of the five, Public Speaking, was described as being "approached on its literary side," with "vocal interpretation of the best literature" a substantial part of the course. English literature seemed bent on devouring its parent. The first literature course as such, now renumbered as English 16, 17, 18, was "designed to cultivate the habit of thoughtful reading and the appreciation of literary form, and to give a general knowledge of the history of English literature." By 1905 the department was called simply English, and the first five courses were called Rhetoric and Composition, English Composition second course, English Composition advanced course, and Argumentative Composition (1 and 2). Only one debate course and two courses in public speaking managed to avoid the word *composition,* and one of these, as we have seen, had a strong literary emphasis. The other old rhetoric courses were all called composition now. The rest was literature, and the courses were organized chronologically, starting with Old English.

Part of this chronicle of the demise of rhetoric is made concrete in Walter Bronson's account of the career of Timothy Whiting Bancroft at Brown. Bronson, who had joined the faculty of English in 1892, wrote a history of Brown in 1914 that is perhaps more useful for its revelations of the author's attitudes than for its information. According to Bronson, in 1883 President Ezekiel Robinson proposed to add a second professor to the English faculty so that English literature and rhetoric might each have its own professor. Alas, it was not to be. Too rash, too premature was Ezekiel. As things developed, Professor Bancroft labored on at the double job until his death in December 1890 from what Bronson, projecting his own feelings, no doubt, called "worry and overwork." We can learn something about the development of "English" from Walter Bronson's chronicle of Bancroft's career:

> The teaching of composition, now the Old Man of
> the Sea to all English Departments, had not then
> quite the same strangling clutch; yet Professor Ban-

croft's reports show that he had to read and correct about one hundred and twenty-five essays and orations monthly, in addition to all his class-room work in rhetoric and literature. He did his best, nevertheless, to meet the growing demand for instruction in English. When the course in English literature was extended in 1874, from half a year to a year, he added a study of individual authors to the survey of the history of the literature; after 1880 he offered an elective in literature in the second half of the senior year; and in 1887–89 he taught a voluntary class in Old English. No man could have done more; and he, at least, ought not to have done so much. (Bronson, 401)

Bronson had been at Brown for eight years when the English department swallowed rhetoric, and fourteen years after that he had the nerve to call composition, which English had taken away from rhetoric, the Old Man of the Sea that held English departments in its strangling clutch.

The brute work of drilling orators and reading compositions had seldom been done by professors but was mainly the work of tutors, instructors, and assistants. Bancroft seems to have been an exception. Certainly Bronson had no such burden. When he came to Brown as an associate professor of English literature, Bronson joined an associate professor of rhetoric and oratory and an associate professor of the English language—but five new instructors came with him, four in English and one in rhetoric. In 1876, Harvard had thwarted an attempt to lure James Francis Child to Johns Hopkins University—by freeing Child of responsibility for correcting compositions. Other schools got the message. But what was happening in such cases needs to be understood in light of the whole shift from an oral and oratorical culture to a culture of the written word, literature, and professionalism. When professors were orators, they did not mind coaching students in oratory. But when professors became philologists, scholars, or literary critics, they deeply resented helping students with a prose that was neither literature nor anything else, but just "composition"—just as students resented and resisted learning a kind of writing that seemed to have no function beyond school.

WORKS CITED

In citing dictionaries and lexicons, I have not given page numbers because the words serve as their own locators. I have also abridged and omitted freely in such citations, in the interests of controlling what still seems at times like an ungainly, though necessary, amount of philological matter. For lengthy quotations from works in foreign languages, I have either used the translations listed below or, where indicated, made my own.

Althusser, Louis. *L'avenir dure longtemps; suivi de, Les faits*. Paris: STOCK/ IMEC, 1992.

Altieri, Charles. "An Idea and Ideal of a Literary Canon." In von Hallberg 1984, 41–64.

Baker, Ernest A. *Cassell's New French Dictionary*. New York: Funk, 1930.

Barthes, Roland. *Image—Music—Text*. Trans. Stephen Heath. New York: Hill and Wang, 1977.

Baxandall, Michael. *Patterns of Intention: On the Historical Explanation of Pictures*. New Haven: Yale University Press, 1985.

Benjamin, Walter. *Illuminationen*. Frankfurt am Main: Suhrkamp, 1961.

———. *Illuminations*. Trans. Harry Zohn. New York: Schocken, 1969.

Benveniste, Emile. *Problems in General Linguistics*. Miami: Miami University Press, 1971.

Berger, John. *Ways of Seeing*. New York: Penguin, 1977.

Bourdieu, Pierre. *Homo Academicus*. Trans. Peter Collier. Stanford: Stanford University Press, 1988.

Brecht, Bertolt. *Brecht on Theatre*. Trans. John Willett. New York: Hill and Wang, 1964.

Bronson, Walter. *The History of Brown University, 1764–1914*. Providence: [Brown] University, 1914.

Brooks, Cleanth. *Modern Poetry and the Tradition*. Chapel Hill: University of North Carolina Press, 1939.

———. *The Well-Wrought Urn*. New York: Harcourt, 1947.

Brooks, Cleanth, and Robert Penn Warren. *Understanding Poetry*. New York: Holt, 1947.

Carlyle, Thomas. *On Heroes, Hero-Worship, and the Heroic in History*. Cincinnati: U. P. James, 1842.

Carr, Edward Hallett. *What Is History?* New York: Vintage, 1961.

Carr, Karen. *The Banalization of Nihilism.* Albany: SUNY Press, 1992.

Catano, James. "Poetry and Computers: Experimenting with the Communal Text." *Computers and the Humanities* 13 (1979), 269–75.

Collingwood, R. G. *The Idea of History.* New York: Oxford University Press, 1956.

Court, Franklin E. *Institutionalizing English Literature: The Culture and Politics of Literary Study, 1750–1900.* Stanford: Stanford University Press, 1992.

Culler, Jonathan. "In Defense of Overinterpretation." In Eco 1992, 109–23.

Delany, Samuel. *Babel-17.* Boston: Gregg, 1976.

de Lauretis, Teresa. *Alice Doesn't: Feminism, Semiotics, Cinema.* Bloomington: Indiana University Press, 1984.

Derrida, Jacques. *Of Grammatology.* Trans. Gayatri Chakravorty Spivak. Baltimore: Johns Hopkins University Press, 1976.

——. *Limited Inc.* Evanston: Northwestern University Press, 1988.

——. "Mochlos; or the Conflict of the Faculties." Trans. Richard Rand and Amy Wygant. In Rand 1992, 1–34.

Donnegan, James. *Greek and English Lexicon.* London: Bohn, 1896.

Doubrovsky, Serge. *The New Criticism in France.* Trans. Derek Coltman. Chicago: University of Chicago Press, 1973.

Eagleton, Terry. *Literary Theory: An Introduction.* Minneapolis: University of Minnesota Press, 1983.

Eco, Umberto, et al. *Interpretation and Overinterpretation.* Cambridge: Cambridge University Press, 1992.

Eliot, T. S. *The Sacred Wood.* London: Methuen, 1960.

Ellis, Havelock. "The Art of Writing." In *The Dance of Life.* New York: Grosset and Dunlap, 1923.

Fish, Stanley. *Professional Correctness: Literary Studies and Political Change.* Oxford: Clarendon, 1995.

Frye, Northrop. *Anatomy of Criticism.* Princeton: Princeton University Press, 1957.

Geertz, Clifford. *The Interpretation of Cultures.* New York: Basic, 1973.

Gerber, John. *The Teaching of English at the University of Iowa,* vol. 1, *The First Hundred Years, 1861–1961.* Iowa City: Maecenas, 1995.

Graff, Gerald. *Professing Literature: An Institutional History.* Chicago: University of Chicago Press, 1987.

Guillory, John. "The Ideology of Canon-Formation: T. S. Eliot and Cleanth Brooks." In von Hallberg 1984, 337–62.

Hegel, G. W. F. *The Philosophy of History.* Trans. J. Sibree. New York: Dover, 1956.

———. *Vorlesungen über die Philosophie der Geschichte.* Stuttgart: Philipp Reclam jun., 1961.

———. *Aesthetics: Lectures on Fine Art.* Trans. T. M. Knox. 2 vols. New York: Oxford University Press, 1975.

———. *Phenomenology of Spirit.* Trans. A. V. Miller. New York: Oxford University Press, 1977.

Holroyd, Michael. *Augustus John: A Biography.* New York: Holt, 1975.

Jameson, Fredric. *The Political Unconscious: Narrative as a Socially Symbolic Act.* Ithaca: Cornell University Press, 1981.

Joyce, James. *Finnegans Wake.* New York: Viking, 1957.

———. *Ulysses.* New York: Random House, 1961.

Kames, Lord [Henry Home]. *Elements of Criticism.* New York: Johnson, 1970.

Keats, John. *Letters of John Keats.* London: Oxford University Press, 1968.

LaCapra, Dominick. *Rethinking Intellectual History.* Ithaca: Cornell University Press, 1983.

Levine, George, ed. *Realism and Representation.* Madison: University of Wisconsin Press, 1993.

Lévi-Strauss, Claude. *Tristes Tropiques.* New York: Atheneum, 1970.

Lewis, Charlton T., and Charles Short. *A Latin Dictionary.* Oxford: Clarendon, 1980.

Liddell, Henry George, and Robert Scott. *Greek-English Lexicon.* Oxford: Clarendon, 1961.

Malson, Lucien. *Wolf Children and the Problem of Human Nature.* New York: Monthly Review Press, 1972.

Miller, Walter James, and Leo Erval Alexandre Saidla. *Engineers as Writers.* Freeport: Books for Libraries, 1974.

Mulvey, Laura. "Visual Pleasure and Narrative Cinema." *Screen* 16, no. 3 (autumn 1975), 6–18.

Nietzsche, Friedrich. *The Birth of Tragedy.* Trans. Walter Kaufmann. New York: Vintage, 1967.

———. *Unzeitgemässe Betrachtungen.* Frankfurt am Main: Insel, 1981.

———. *Untimely Meditations.* Trans. R. J. Hollingdale. Cambridge: Cambridge University Press, 1983.

Ohmann, Richard. *English in America: A Radical View of the Profession.* New York: Oxford University Press, 1976.

———. "The Shaping of a Canon: U.S. Fiction, 1960–1975." In von Hallberg 1984, 377–401.

Oxford English Dictionary. New York: Oxford University Press, 1971.

Peirce, Charles Sanders. *Philosophical Writings of Peirce.* Ed. Justus Buchler. New York: Dover, 1955.

Phelps, William Lyon. *Autobiography with Letters.* New York: Oxford University Press, 1939.

Pierson, George Wilson. *Yale College: An Educational History, 1871–1921.* New Haven: Yale University Press, 1952.

———. *A Yale Book of Numbers: Historical Statistics of the College and University, 1701–1976.* New Haven: Yale University, 1983.

Rand, Richard, ed. *Logomachia: The Conflict of the Faculties.* Lincoln: University of Nebraska Press, 1992.

Rorty, Richard. *Philosophical Papers,* vols. 1 and 2. Cambridge: Cambridge University Press, 1991.

———. "The Pragmatist's Progress." In Eco 1992, 89–108.

———. "A Comment on Robert Scholes's 'Tlön and Truth.'" In Levine 1993, 186–89.

Ruskin, John. *Unto This Last.* New York: Appleton-Century-Crofts, 1967.

Sartre, Jean-Paul. *What Is Literature?* New York: Harper and Row, 1965.

Saussure, Ferdinand de. *Course in General Linguistics.* Trans. Wade Baskin. New York: McGraw-Hill, 1966.

Scholes, Robert. *Textual Power.* New Haven: Yale University Press, 1985.

———. *Protocols of Reading.* New Haven: Yale University Press, 1989.

———. "Tlön and Truth: Reflections on Literary Theory and Philosophy." In Levine 1993, 169–85.

Scholes, Robert, and Nancy R. Comley. *The Practice of Writing.* New York: St. Martin's, 1981, rev. eds. 1985, 1989, 1994.

Scholes, Robert, Nancy R. Comley, and Gregory L. Ulmer. *Text Book.* New York: St. Martin's, 1988, rev. ed. 1995.

Scholes, Robert, and Robert Kellogg. *The Nature of Narrative.* New York: Oxford University Press, 1966.

Searle, John R. *The Construction of Social Reality.* New York: Free Press, 1995.

Shattuck, Roger. *The Forbidden Experiment: The Story of the Wild Boy of Aveyron.* New York: Washington Square, 1980.

Spender, Dale. *Man Made Language.* London: Routledge, 1980.

von Hallberg, Robert. *Canons.* Chicago: University of Chicago Press, 1984.

White, Hayden. *Tropics of Discourse.* Baltimore: Johns Hopkins University Press, 1978.

Young, Robert. "The Idea of a Chrestomatic University." In Rand 1992, 97–126.

INDEX